The Problematic Self
in
Kierkegaard and Freud

The Problematic Self

in

Kierkegaard and Freud

by J. Preston Cole

New Haven and London, Yale University Press, 1971

Designed by Marvin Howard Simmons
and set in IBM Press Roman type.
Printed in the United States of America by
The Carl Purington Rollins Printing-Office of
The Yale University Press, New Haven, Connecticut.

Distributed in Great Britain, Europe, and Africa by
Yale University Press, Ltd., London; in Canada by
McGill-Queen's University Press, Montreal; in Mexico
by Centro Interamericano de Libros Académicos,
Mexico City; in Central and South America by Kaiman
& Polon, Inc., New York City; in Australasia by
Australia and New Zealand Book Co., Pty., Ltd.,
Artarmon, New South Wales; in India by UBS Publishers'
Distributors Pvt., Ltd., Delhi; in Japan by John
Weatherhill, Inc., Tokyo.

To Donna,
without whom my selfhood
would be impoverished.

Contents

Abbreviations

Kierkegaard References

CoD	*The Concept of Dread.* Princeton: Princeton University Press, 1957.
CUP	*Concluding Unscientific Postscript to the Philosophical Fragments.* Princeton: Princeton University Press, 1941.
E/O	*Either/Or.* Garden City, N.Y.: Doubleday & Company, Anchor Books, 1959.
F&T	*Fear and Trembling.* Garden City, N.Y.: Doubleday & Company, Anchor Books, 1954.
Jour	*The Journals of Kierkegaard.* Edited by Alexander Dru. London: Oxford University Press, 1938.
PF	*Philosophical Fragments, or a Fragment of Philosophy.* Princeton: Princeton University Press, 1958.
PoV	*The Point of View for My Work as an Author.* New York: Harper & Row, Torchbooks, 1962.
Rep	*Repetition: An Essay in Experimental Psychology.* Princeton: Princeton University Press, 1941.
SuD	*Sickness unto Death.* Garden City, N.Y.: Doubleday & Company, Anchor Books, 1954.
TiC	*Training in Christianity.* Princeton: Princeton University Press, 1947.

Freud References

BPP	*Beyond the Pleasure Principle.* New York: Bantam Books, 1959.

C&D	*Civilization and Its Discontents.* Garden City, N.Y.: Doubleday & Company, Anchor Books, 1958.
CP I-V	*Collected Papers.* Edited by J. Riviere and J. Strachey. London: Hogarth Press, 1957.
E&I	*The Ego and the Id.* London: Hogarth Press, 1957.
FoI	*The Future of an Illusion.* Garden City, N.Y.: Doubleday & Company, Anchor Books, 1957.
GIP	*A General Introduction to Psychoanalysis.* New York: Washington Square Press, 1960.
GP&AE	*Group Psychology and the Analysis of the Ego.* New York: Bantam Books, 1960.
IoD	*The Interpretation of Dreams* in *The Basic Writings of Sigmund Freud.* Edited by A. A. Brill. New York: Random House, Modern Library, 1938.
M&M	*Moses and Monotheism.* New York: Alfred A. Knopf, Vintage Books, 1959.
NIL	*New Introductory Lectures on Psychoanalysis.* New York: W. W. Norton & Company, 1933.
PoA	*The Problem of Anxiety.* New York: W. W. Norton & Company, 1936.
SiH	*Studies in Hysteria.* Boston: Beacon Press, 1937.
TCTS	*Three Contributions to the Theory of Sex* in *The Basic Writings of Sigmund Freud.* Edited by A. A. Brill. New York: Random House, Modern Library, 1938.

Introduction: Human Nature and the Historicity of Selfhood

The problem of the self has proven to be a most persistent one. It is an enigma which has puzzled the most perceptive observers, perhaps the wisest of whom have been content to leave the self a mystery. But there are some whose curiosity— or perhaps compassion—overrides their prudence, and these have sought to unravel the riddle of the self. If it is wiser to let the mystery remain, the problem itself will not be denied. It is a perennial problem which emerges periodically with compelling necessity, for it is man's most intimate and therefore most significant problem. Martin Buber has noted that the problem emerges at times of "cosmic homelessness," times when the structures of meaning which bring cosmos out of chaos begin to crumble. When the metaphysical home in which man dwells secure begins to collapse, the problem of the self reappears with all its existential urgency. Thrown back on his own resources, man asks in desperation, "Who am I?"

Buber points to Socrates, Augustine, Pascal, and Kant as the great existential interrogators; and to Aristotle, Thomas Aquinas, Spinoza, and Hegel as the edifice builders by means of which the problem of the self has been periodically laid to rest. He concludes, however, that since Kant the question cannot be surpressed. No cosmic home is possible, as Hegel's short-lived experiment confirmed. "No new house in the universe is being planned for man, but he, as the builder of houses, is being required to know himself," Buber says.[1]

1. Martin Buber, *Between Man and Man* (London: Macmillan & Company, 1957), p. 137.

This is the task which the generations since Kant have set for themselves. But the tools appropriate for the task have not been ready at hand. We have had to forge the tools which make possible the analysis of the self.

Actually, Kant represents the culmination of a critical line of thought which leads from Locke through Berkeley and Hume, and which resulted in the destruction of rationalistic psychology. Coincident with this critical line of inquiry, however, was the constructive effort to develop a "science of human nature" whose principles and methods were patterned after those of the natural sciences. If such methods had proven useful in the study of nature, why not apply them to the problem of *human* nature? And so, for over two centuries the inquiry into the nature of the self proceeded on a mechanistic basis, grounded in a naturalistic ontology.

But the concept of nature is not a constant; it has a history, as R. G. Collingwood has pointed out.[2] By the middle of the nineteenth century another conception of nature had emerged, a conception which might be called a "vitalistic" view of nature. It grew out of the failure of mechanistic naturalism to deal adequately with the problem of becoming. In a sense, vitalistic naturalism is as old as Aristotle, but it emerged in the nineteenth century in the guise of evolution. It was not long before the problem of the self was being attacked with renewed vigor with tools derived from the biological sciences. Here we look to such men as Spencer and Galton, who are of course indebted to Darwin and Lamarck, and to a more intuitive group of thinkers, who equally sought to understand the self in terms of some vitalistic principle—men like Schopenhauer, von Hartmann, Nietzsche, and Bergson.

It was into this setting that the man who has perhaps done more than any other to fathom the mystery of the self appeared—Sigmund Freud. Eclectically he borrowed their ideas,

2. R. G. Collingwood, *The Idea of History* (New York: Oxford University Press, Galaxy Books, 1957). See especially the essay "Human Nature and Human History," pp. 205-31.

modifying, revising, and welding them together into a coherent view of man. His early work reveals how much he is dependent upon the mechanistic view of nature. Adopting the methods which had served the physical sciences so well, he sought to construct a mechanistic model of the self, but with little success. Freud's fidelity to his clinical observations, however, soon forced him to seek a new model, and he turned to the emerging biologistic model of vitalistic naturalism. Here his indebtedness to Darwin, Spencer, and Galton, as well as Schopenhauer and von Hartmann, becomes apparent. He is really a product of both traditions. He borrows freely from the conceptual warehouse of each, without being bound to the theoretical systems produced by either. A natural child of both the mechanistic and the vitalistic traditions, Freud displays filial obeisance to neither.

The result is a brilliant interpretation of the dynamics of selfhood which has clearly demonstrated its usefulness in untangling the snarls people make of their lives. Nevertheless, while clarifying many of the mysteries in the problem of the self, Freud's analysis seems to distort the reality of human existence at many points. His reduction of selfhood to a function of the sex drive seems inadequate to many—even to those who are not at all victims of Victorian superegos. The radical determinism which underlies his method appears a half-truth to many sensitive students of the self—even to some who are profoundly aware of the bondage of the self.

It is the thesis of this essay that these and other similar difficulties are the result of Freud's attempt to express the *historical* reality of human existence within a *naturalistic* framework. A naturalistic ontology imposes considerable limitations when used as a vehicle for comprehending an historical reality. Freud's shift from the mechanistic to the vitalistic model of nature is indicative of his quest for an adequate conceptuality. But, while the vitalistic model is much more amenable to his subject matter, it also vitiates the essential historicity of selfhood. To his credit and our frustration, he continually revised his concepts, thus seeking to break out of the psychological into what he liked to call the "metapsychological."

It is my belief that Freud would have benefited from a more appropriate conceptuality. The historicity of man can never be adequately conceptualized in the categories of nature, whether they are construed mechanistically or vitalistically. To a degree these are helpful ways of conceiving human existence, for of course man is both a physical being and a biological being. But, to the degree that man is able to transcend his nature and create a history, the naturalistic methodology is of limited utility. What is needed is a radical shift from a naturalistic to an historical ontology. Fortunately, there is one student of the self who has sought to understand man historically rather than naturalistically. This man is Søren Kierkegaard. From his studies of the self we may gain some insight into the utility of an historical ontology in understanding human existence.

Kierkegaard, no less than Freud, was saddled with an inappropriate conceptual framework for his task. Where Freud was struggling to be free from the confinement of mechanistic naturalism, Kierkegaard was in revolt against Hegelian idealism. Kierkegaard was a vigorous opponent of Hegelianism, but his thought was shaped by the very thought forms he attacked. He is both the product of his age and its opponent. We must see him as a corrective to his time rather than as an innovator, though, in a way, his corrective became an innovation. Both Kierkegaard and Hegel are dialectical thinkers, but Hegel's is a closed dialectic and Kierkegaard's is continually open. Both understand selfhood as a dialectical synthesis of Nature and Spirit. But in Hegel the synthesis transpires with necessity, while in Kierkegaard the synthesis depends upon the individual's existential decision. For both, the essence of man is Spirit. But in Hegel the very life of Spirit is crushed out by the necessity of the System, while in Kierkegaard the synthesis is sustained only in the free response of faith. As Kierkegaard points out, the System founders upon the stubborn fact of freedom. In short, we could say that Kierkegaard is a protest from within the idealist milieu on behalf of the self.

The ontology with which he emerged is precisely the historical ontology which Freud needed in his attempt to give adequate expression to his insights into human existence. Spirit, if I may use the term with reference to Freud, has a very difficult time finding articulation. Within the deterministic structure of the naturalistic ontology, there was simply no place for such a notion. And yet Freud's analysis of the human situation required some recognition of human freedom. Freud was never able to break free from the naturalistic thought forms of his age. Yet, almost in spite of himself, the fact of human freedom found expression. Within the limitations of his conceptual framework, the notion of Spirit emerges only in a crippled and distorted form, but it nevertheless manages to claim from Freud some recognition.

Freud was never introduced to the work of Kierkegaard but, since we have before us Kierkegaard's own sensitive analysis of the self, developed on the basis of an historical ontology, it is worthwhile to compare these two seminal studies. The comparison may seem rash, for two more dissimilar persons than the objective scientist and the passionate theologian would be difficult to find. The one is quite apparently a Greek in his presuppositions, a child of the Enlightenment, a man of reason. The other belongs to the Judeo-Christian tradition, a rebellious child of idealism, a man of faith. Yet, as one of the few who has attempted such a comparison has put it,

> They confirm each other in their conclusions; they criticize each other in their limitations; and they match each other perfectly. Those aspects omitted by the one are brilliantly treated by the other, and rarely in the history of thought have two thinkers explored a common problem so thoroughly in entirely different manners, so that the efforts of both represent a grandiose whole.[3]

3. F. J. Hacker, "Freud, Marx, and Kierkegaard," in *Freud and the*

I intend to penetrate the conceptual structures in which both Freud and Kierkegaard seek to communicate their understanding of the character of human existence and to demonstrate the similarity of their insight which is otherwise disguised in the conceptual forms of vitalistic naturalism and the remnants of philosophical idealism. In a sense, what I am saying is that both Freud's naturalistic categories and Kierkegaard's idealistic categories are ultimately inadequate to comprehend the complexities of human existence. I am not proposing a third alternative, but merely suggesting that through the fortunate circumstance of having two such different perspectives on the same phenomenon we are blessed with a kind of binocular vision which may permit us to have something of a three-dimensional view of man.

The structure of this study is that of classical Christian anthropology. That is, it proceeds through three aspects of existence—creation, fall, and salvation—in sections I have entitled: "The Dialectic of Selfhood," "The Loss of Selfhood," and "The Restoration of Selfhood." Within each of the three parts I seek to give an exhaustive study, first, of Kierkegaard's treatment of the subject, and then of Freud's, before proceeding to my own attempt to construct a binoptic synthesis in what I call an "interpolation."

Part One sets forth Kierkegaard's doctrine of Spirit as the power of selfhood, comparing it with Freud's Libido concept. Kierkegaard's concept of the self is compared with Freud's concept of the ego. And Kierkegaard's "stages on life's way"—the aesthetic, the ethical, and the religious—are compared with Freud's treatment of the evolution of the self from an id, through the development of the ego and the superego.

In Part Two, each writer's concept of a "fall" is examined. Kierkegaard's "dreaming innocence" is compared with Freud's notion of "infantile sexuality." Kierkegaard's concept of

---

20th Century, ed. Benjamin Nelson (New York: Meridian Books, 1957), p. 126.

dread, which is the presupposition of the fall into despair, is compared with Freud's notion of anxiety as the presupposition of repression, which produces neurosis. And Kierkegaard's notion of sin and the demoniacal are compared with Freud's treatment of neurosis and psychosis.

Part Three deals with the therapeutic problem. Here, Freud's psychotherapy, which is grounded in a naturalistic ontology, is compared with Kierkegaard's "Christian therapeutic," which is grounded in an historical ontology. Freud's therapeutic theory is given a detailed comparison with Kierkegaard's "double movement of the spirit," which includes resignation and faith.

Finally, the implications for psychoanalysis and for theology are explored in the concluding chapter.

The studies of Freud and Kierkegaard are exhaustive, and the interpolations seek to illumine the concepts of each in the light of the other. It is hoped that in this way new light has been thrown on both Freud and Kierkegaard, or that at least Kierkegaard will have been made intelligible to Freudians, and Freud to Kierkegaardians, who seem eternally at war.

Part One
The Dialectic of
Selfhood

1. Kierkegaard's Concept of the Self

(1)

Spirit: The Power of Selfhood

One of the most enigmatic paragraphs in the entire Kierke-gaardian corpus is found in the opening pages of his little classic, *The Sickness unto Death*. In a style that reveals his mastery of the Hegelian dialectic, he sets forth his definition of man.

> Man is spirit. But what is spirit? Spirit is the self. But what is the self? The self is a relation which relates itself to its own self, or it is that in the relation [which accounts for it] that the relation relates itself to its own self; the self is not the relation but [consists in the fact] that the relation relates itself to its own self. Man is a synthesis of the infinite and the finite, of the temporal and the eternal, of freedom and necessity, in short it is a synthesis. A synthesis is a relation between two factors. So regarded, man is not yet a self. [*SuD*, 146]

This piece of finely spun rhetoric is the equal of anything in Hegel—but with a difference. The involved definition of the self concludes with the irony that sets the men apart: "So regarded, man is not yet a self." With this gesture Kierkegaard turns the definition into a riddle, to the resolution of which he devotes the entire volume. If we are to grasp his understanding of the self, we must unravel that riddle. And if we are to unravel the riddle, we must take seriously both the dialectical logic and the ironic fillip.

11

"The self is a relation" implies that the self is comprised of
at least two elements, and for Kierkegaard these basic components are the classical concepts of body and soul. Here *body*
signifies the physical aspect of human being, and *soul* the
affective or psychological aspect. So regarded, man would be
construed as an immediate relationship between body and
soul, the physical and the psychological. To be sure he is this,
but as such he is not yet a self. Such a being is only an "it," or
at best a "me"—a self "in the dative case," as Kierkegaard
expresses it elsewhere. "The *immediate* man . . . is merely soulishly determined, his self or he himself is a something included
along with 'the other' . . . wishing, desiring, enjoying, etc., but
passively. . . . Its dialectic is: the agreeable and the disagreeable" (*SuD*, 184).

Indeed, the immediate body-soul relation is not really a relation, but a unity—a psychosomatic unity, so to speak. It is a
"negative unity," as Kierkegaard terms it, but selfhood requires a positive relationship, one posited by the self itself. In
short, while man is a relationship of body and soul, that relationship is not yet the self. But, "if on the contrary the relation relates itself to its own self, the relation is then the positive third term, and this is the self" (*SuD*, 146).

So the initial definition of the self must be qualified. "The
self is a relation which relates *itself* to its own self" (*SuD*, 146;
italics mine). This is an entirely different mode of being from
that of the immediate body-soul unity. It is the distinctively
human mode of being. The immediate relation of the body-
soul unity is a passive mode of being. It does not determine its
own actions, but it is itself determined. It does not act, but it
is acted upon. It does not live its own life but is lived by its
own passions. Selfhood, on the other hand, is that mode of
being in which the individual assumes responsibility for itself.
The relation takes up a relation to its own self. It does not
negate the immediate relation but mediates the relation, thereby elevating it into a new kind of being.

At this point a rather fundamental question, that of the

dynamic whereby the self becomes a self, arises. Is the self autonomous? Can the immediate self become a genuine self of its own power, or does the self owe its existence to some other power? Is the relation of selfhood self-constituted, or is it constituted by another?

To give Kierkegaard's answer to this question, I must anticipate a concept with which I shall deal at length in Part Two, the notion of despair. If selfhood constitutes the truly human mode of being, then despair is nonbeing. Kierkegaard distinguishes two kinds of despair at the level of consciousness. The first is the "despair of weakness," wherein the individual is too weak to assume responsibility for himself and so does not become a self. The second is the "despair of defiance," wherein the individual refuses to assume responsibility for himself and likewise does not become a self. Now Kierkegaard notes, "If the human self had constituted itself, there could be a question only of one form [of despair], that of not willing to be one's own self, . . . but there would be no question of despairingly willing to be oneself" (*SuD*, 147).

The first form of despair is quite understandable on the thesis that men are autonomous or self-constituted selves. They remain in despair because they simply will not make the effort. But the second form is incomprehensible on this thesis. It is the ironic form of despair, for in the very act of rejecting selfhood the individual must affirm his selfhood, thereby disclosing his dependence upon the very thing he would reject. As Kierkegaard spells it out:

> A despairing man wants despairingly to be himself. . . .
> That self which he despairingly wills to be is a self which
> he is not . . . ; what he really wills is to tear his self away
> from the Power which constituted it. But notwithstanding
> all his despair, that Power is the stronger, and it compels
> him to be the self he does not will to be. [*SuD*, 153]

The self, then, is not simply self-constituted but is constituted by another. Selfhood is contingent upon a third factor, a

Power which is not identical with either body or soul. When the self relates itself to its immediate self, the essential elements of selfhood, i.e. body and soul, are not related in passive unity but in a dynamic way that constitutes a genuinely new mode of being. When this mode obtains, body and soul are no longer immediately related but are mediated by a new entity, the self; and this self "is grounded transparently in the Power which posited it" (*SuD*, 147). Conversely, when this relationship does not obtain, and a disrelation in the relationship develops, the self does not exist. The breakdown does not occur in the immediate body-soul relationship but in the mediated relationship, and since the self is the mediate relationship it no longer exists. It is no longer grounded in the Power which constitutes it. In Kierkegaard's words,

> The disrelationship of despair is not a simple disrelationship but a disrelationship in a relation which relates itself to its own self and is constituted by another, so that the disrelationship in that self-relation reflects itself infinitely in relation to the Power which constituted it. [*SuD*, 147]

This Power, then, is the Power of selfhood, or the Power of being, for the self is contingent upon it. Insofar as the self is grounded in this Power, it exists; and insofar as it is not, it does not exist. Hence, this Power is truly the Power of being for the self, and the relationship to this Power is a matter of being and not being for the self.

Kierkegaard called this Power *Spirit*. It constitutes the third essential element of selfhood. In *The Concept of Dread* he put it this way: "Man is a synthesis of the soulish and the bodily. But a synthesis is unthinkable if the two are not united in a third factor. This third factor is the spirit" (*CoD*, 39). Now, Spirit, as the Power of human being, is given with human existence. It is present in man from the beginning as a possibility to be actualized. Even in the primal state of man, Spirit is present as the potential third term in the relationship which positively relates body and soul. Kierkegaard states, "In the state of innocence man is not merely an animal, for if at any time of his life he was merely an animal, he never would become a man. So then the spirit is present, but in a state of immediacy, a dreaming state" (*CoD*, 39). But in this primal state, man is not yet a self. He is still an "it." His existence is still immediately determined by his natural drives. Selfhood is as yet only a possibility. In Kierkegaard's words, "In his innocence man is not determined as spirit but is soulishly determined in immediate unity with his natural condition. Spirit is dreaming in man" (*CoD*, 37).

In this quiescent state there arises that which disturbs this immediate relation. This disturbance is due to the presence of Spirit. "Dreamingly the spirit projects its own reality" (*CoD*, 38), which is the true reality of man. To the immediate self, which is determined by its own natural desires or drives, there comes the awareness of another mode of being peculiar to man. Dreamingly, Spirit becomes manifest to the individual as a possibility, *his* possibility. Thus his true being, Spirit, is projected as his own reality, an unrealized reality, a reality which is as yet only a possibility.

In a sense, Spirit is "a hostile power, for it constantly disturbs the relation between soul and body" (*CoD*, 39). But, as we have seen, this immediate relation is not yet a self. It only becomes a self when a relationship is posited in which the self relates itself to its own self. Since this is precisely the function of Spirit, it is also a "friendly power." Without this projected reality, man would have no perception of his true mode of being. Spirit is, therefore, an "ambiguous power," which threatens the placid coexistence of body and soul and yet makes possible their real relationship, their synthesis. This synthesis does not transpire with necessity but always in freedom, for a synthesis which transpires by necessity is still an "it" and not an "I." Only the self which actualizes *itself* is truly an "I." But, while the actual synthesis does not transpire with necessity, the possibility is always present. Spirit is a relentless possibility for man, and its reality is independent of the self, but its actualization is contingent upon the action of the self. And this actualization is a task which never ends.

In summary, then, the elements which comprise Kierkegaard's concept of the self are three: body, soul, and Spirit. The body is the physical aspect of the self; the soul is the affective or psychological aspect; and the Spirit is the relational or dialectical aspect. In the primal state of being, body and soul are related in immediate unity. Man is soulishly determined in immediate unity with the body—which is to say, his existence is determined by his psychological needs. Latent within this body-soul unity, however, is Spirit, the possibility of self-determination. Spirit continually projects itself as a possible mode of being, disturbing the passive unity of the psychosomatic entity, and tempting it to become responsible for itself. When the relation actualizes this possibility it has made the transition from an "it" to an "I"; it has become a self. But the danger of losing the selfhood thus actualized is an ever-present possibility. The relationship which constitutes selfhood, then, persists only so long as the self continues to actualize the possibility which Spirit projects.

So, to return to the enigmatic definition of the self with which we began our investigation, "The self is a relation which relates itself to its own self. . . . The self is not the relation but consists in the fact that the relation relates itself to its own self" (*SuD*, 146). In other words, the self is not the immediate relation of body and soul but consists in the fact that this immediate relation relates itself to its own self. The Power which makes possible this mediated relationship is Spirit. Selfhood, then, is a dialectical concept; a dialectic of the Spirit, to which Kierkegaard gives careful attention.

The Finite and the Infinite

Again, let us use Kierkegaard's involutional definition as our starting point. "Man is a synthesis of the infinite and the finite, of the temporal and the eternal, of freedom and necessity" (*SuD*, 146). This threefold synthesis does not signify three separate relationships but three aspects of a single dialectic. The central dialectic of selfhood is the relation between the body-soul entity and Spirit, the Power of being. In the formula quoted above, the finite, the temporal, and the necessary represent the body-soul element in the dialectic, and the infinite, the eternal, and the possible represent the spiritual element in the dialectic.[1] Under the aspects of the finite and the infinite Kierkegaard discusses the dialectic of selfhood with respect to its essential structure; under the aspects of necessity and possibility he discusses the dialectic of selfhood with respect to its existential becoming; and under the aspects of the temporal and the eternal he discusses the dialectic of selfhood with respect to its qualitative norm. I shall call the first the *essential dialectic*, the second the *existential dialectic*, and the third the *eternal dialectic*.

Discussing the self as a dialectical relation between the finite and the infinite, Kierkegaard says, "The self is the conscious synthesis of infinitude and finitude which relates itself to itself, whose task is to become itself, a task which can be performed only by means of a relationship to God" (*SuD*, 162). The essential elements in the dialectic are those I have already noted. The body-soul entity is the finite element, and the Spirit is the infinite element. "The self is a synthesis in which the finite is the limiting factor, and the infinite is the expanding factor" (*SuD*, 163). Or, again, the dialectic of selfhood "consists in moving away from oneself infinitely by the process of infinitizing oneself, and in returning to oneself infinitely by the process of finitizing" (*SuD*, 162-63). The dialectic of Spirit, then, is the process whereby the infinite possibilities of selfhood are disclosed to the finite, immediate self. In this process the immediate self is made aware of ever new horizons of selfhood.

1. Kierkegaard customarily employs the term *possibility* in conjunction with *necessity*, though the connotation of *freedom* is certainly preserved. Throughout my discussion I shall employ the former.

The instrument through which Spirit accomplishes this expansive function is the imagination, as Kierkegaard notes. "Imagination is the medium of the process of infinitizing" (*SuD,* 163). Through imagination Spirit projects the abstract possibilities of the self; it "images" the self which the immediate self might be. "The self is reflection," Kierkegaard says, "and imagination is reflection, it is the counterfeit presentment of the self, which is the possibility of the self" (*SuD,* 164). That is to say, the imagination is the capacity of the self to mirror an image of itself, to project a picture of the possible self. It is this ability which creates the other pole of the dialectic of selfhood, the transcendent, infinite self, as against the immediate, finite self. Note, however, that this image is not a mirror-image of the self. It is a "counterfeit presentment of the self." And yet it is the possibility of the self—the self one is not yet, the transcendent self. It is an imaged possibility in dialectical relation with which the individual exists.

Thus, imagination is crucial to the dialectic of selfhood. Whatever feeling, knowledge, or will a man has ultimately depends upon imagination. But Kierkegaard hastens to warn that while the finite self does not in itself constitute selfhood, neither is this infinite or transcendent self the real self. He insists that the self is a dialectical relation between the two. If one becomes infatuated with the transcendent self and mistakes it for the real self, then the imagination has become fantastic. It has infinitized the self out of all relation to the finite self. It has carried possibility to the point of impossibility. Kierkegaard illustrates this with regard to feeling, knowledge, and will.

> When feeling becomes fantastic, the self is simply volatilized more and more, at last becoming a sort of abstract sentimentality which is so inhuman that it does not apply to any person, but inhumanly participates feelingly, so to speak, in the fate of one or another abstraction, e.g. that of mankind *in abstracto....* So it is with him whose feel-

> ing has become fantastic; he becomes in a way infinitized,
> but not in such a way that he becomes more and more
> himself, for he loses himself more and more. [*SuD*, 164]

Again, with respect to knowledge, the self may become fantastic.

> The law for the development of the self with respect to
> knowledge, in so far as it is true that the self becomes
> itself, is this, that the increasing degree of knowledge cor-
> responds with the degree of self-knowledge, that the more
> the self knows, the more it knows itself. If this does not
> occur, then the more knowledge increases, the more it
> becomes a kind of inhuman knowing for the production of
> which man's self is squandered. [*SuD*, 164]

And so also with respect to the will: "When the will becomes
fantastic, the self likewise is volatilized more and more" (*SuD*,
164). One may lose himself in the fantastic if his resolve to do
great things is not kept in dialectical relation with a resolve to
do that finite portion of the project which is immediately at
hand. To be a concrete self the will must

> constantly become concrete in the same degree that it is
> abstract, in such a way that the more it is infinitized in
> purpose and resolution, the more present and contempo-
> raneous with itself does it become in the small part of the
> task which can be realized at once, so that in being infini-
> tized it returns in the strictest sense to its self. [*SuD*,
> 164-65]

When feeling, or knowledge, or will becomes fantastic, the
self loses itself in its striving after infinity, i.e. after indeterminateness. But the dialectical self can also be lost if it contents itself with the immediate, the determinate, the finite. To
exist without the finite dimension is fantastic and illusory, but
the correlate danger is that of finitude in which the transcendent dimension of human existence has been lost. Here

the self is lost "not by evaporation in the infinite, but by being entirely finitized, by having become, instead of a self, a number, just one man more, one more repetition of the everlasting *Einerlei*" (*SuD*, 166). The finite man allows the crowd to define what it means to be a man. He loses his self in conformity to his culture's criterion of human existence. Of course, by his culture's standards he is precisely what a man ought to be. But in a deeper sense he has lost his self. He has "become an imitation, a number, a cipher in the crowd" (*SuD*, 167).

Thus a dialectic must be sustained between the finite and the infinite, between the finite self each man is and the infinite possibility of selfhood. It is such a dialectic that Spirit makes possible. Through the medium of imagination, Spirit is able to project a transcendent image of the self. To live concretely in dialectical relation with this transcendent self is the task of selfhood.

Kierkegaard understands this task to be essentially a theological one. As we noted earlier, he says, "The self is the conscious synthesis of infinitude and finitude which relates itself to itself, whose task is to become itself, a task which can be performed only by means of a relationship to God" (*SuD*, 162). The dialectical relationship of the finite immediate self with the projected image of the self Kierkegaard calls a "God-relationship." This is not to say that the imaged self is God. It would be more accurate to say that Spirit is Kierkegaard's God-concept. But the dialectical relation of the finite self with the infinite self defines the way in which the God-concept functions in the dialectic of selfhood. Spirit, or God, receives specificity in the image of selfhood which it projects. This image functions as a god to the self. Certainly our projected images of the self are not identical with God. They are in fact idols, graven images, counterfeit gods. But existence in relation to the transcendent self is a relationship in which the imaged self functions as a god.

We can now see what Kierkegaard means when he says, "the God-relationship infinitizes" (*SuD*, 165). It is by virtue of the projected image of the self that the self is enabled to transcend the finite immediate self. By virtue of a God-concept, however imperfect it may be, the determinate character of the immediate self is at least partially overcome, and the self "is grounded transparently in the Power which constituted it" (*SuD*, 147). Thus the task of becoming a self is impossible apart from the God-relationship.

Necessity and Possibility

The foregoing discussion has been concerned only with the essentialist question, i.e. the essence of selfhood; it has not dealt with the existential question, i.e. the transition from essence to existence. Essentially the self is a relation between the finite and the infinite, but how does it become what it essentially is? It is with this hiatus, between the self man is but is not and the self he is not but is, that Kierkegaard is preoccupied. The transition from the immediate self to the mediate self, which logic so beautifully negotiates but on which existence founders, is his major concern. This pause in the flow of logic is for him a lifetime.

Kierkegaard gives careful consideration to the logical problem involved in becoming a self in the "Interlude" which he introduces into his *Philosophical Fragments,* and to the existential problem in his discussion of the dialectic of necessity and possibility in *The Sickness unto Death.* In the former he asks, "How does that which comes into being change? Or, what is the nature of the change involved in becoming?" (*PF,* 60). Here he distinguishes two kinds of change, *alloiosis* and *kinesis. Alloiosis* is a qualitative change, a change in essence, and *kinesis* is a change in the mode of being. Becoming is not a change in essence, he reasons, "for if the subject of becoming does not in itself remain unchanged in the process of becoming, it is not *this* which comes into being, but some other thing, and the question is guilty of a μετάβασις εἰς ἄλλο γένος" (*PF,* 60). Thus, becoming "is clearly not a change in essence, but in being; it is a transition from not being to being" (*PF*, 60). So then, the change involved in becoming a self is not a change in essence but a change in existence. The essence of selfhood remains the same, but the change is from nonbeing to being.

"But," Kierkegaard continues, "this non-being which the subject of becoming leaves behind must itself have some sort of being" (*PF*, 60), otherwise it could not legitimately be called a becoming, since, as we have seen, becoming presupposes a something which comes into being. He concludes,

> A being, of this kind, which is nevertheless a non-being, is what we know as possibility; and a being which is being is actual being, or actuality; so that the change involved in becoming is the transition from possibility to actuality. [*PF*, 60]

Now the question is: how does this transition take place, by necessity or with freedom? Kierkegaard insists that nothing ever comes into being by necessity. "The necessary . . . is not a determination of being but of essence, since it is of the essence of the necessary to be"(*PF*, 61). Necessity has to do with the essence of a thing; possibility and actuality with its existence. It is a confusion of terms to speak of a necessary transition from possibility to actuality. He concludes:

> The transition takes place with freedom. Becoming is never necessary. It was not necessary before it came into being, for then it could not come into being; nor after it came into being, for then it has not come into being. [*PF*, 61]

Thus, becoming is the unity of possibility and necessity—the unity of an essence which *is* by necessity, with possibility as its existential qualification. Only when an abstract essence is united with possibility can it become actual.

This is the logic of all becoming, but Kierkegaard makes a distinction between two kinds of becoming. The "first becom-

ing" is a natural process; the "second becoming" is an historical process. The former applies to the immediate self, while
the latter applies to the mediate self. In reality, even the natural becoming is historical, for as we have seen, the transition
from possibility to actuality takes place only with freedom.
Thus nature is history in the mode of actuality. It is actualized
possibility. But in the realm of human existence there is the
possibility of a "second becoming within the first becoming,"
as Kierkegaard puts it.

> Here we have the historical in the stricter sense, subject to
> a dialectic with respect to time. The becoming which in
> this sphere is identical with the becoming of nature is a
> possibility, a possibility which for nature is its whole reali-
> ty. But this historical becoming in the stricter sense is a
> becoming within a becoming, which should constantly be
> kept in mind. The more specifically historical becoming
> comes into being by the operation of a relatively free
> cause, which in turn points ultimately to an absolutely free
> cause. [*PF*, 62]

Thus, whereas the first becoming takes place by nature, the
second becoming takes place historically; whereas the immediate self comes into being by nature, the mediate self comes
into being historically, i.e. by the relatively free act of the
subject itself. But we must not forget that even the first becoming is ultimately historical and that the very possibility of
selfhood is for nature its whole reality.

Kierkegaard sets forth the logic of the self as a relation between necessity and possibility as follows:

> When the self as a synthesis of finitude and infinitude is
> once constituted, when already it *is* κατὰ δύναμιν, then in
> order to *become* it reflects itself in the medium of imagi-
> nation, and with that the infinite possibility comes into
> view. The self κατὰ δύναμιν is just as possible as it is neces-
> sary; for though it is itself, it has to become itself. Inas-

much as it is itself, it is the necessary, and inasmuch as it has to become itself, it is a possibility. [*SuD*, 168]

The self is essentially a relation between the finite and the infinite—between the finite, immediate self and its infinite possibilities. This is the self κατα δυναμιν, but it does not become actual with necessity. The relationship which constitutes the necessary essence of the self becomes actual only with the addition of possibility, i.e. in freedom. Thus the self, which was structurally seen to be a relation between the finite and the infinite, is dynamically seen to be a relation between necessity and possibility.

Here, even as in the dialectic of finitude and infinitude, one can lose his self if he loses either pole of the dialectic. The self can be lost in the possible if it loses its relation to the self it necessarily is. What the self is to become is not just any possibility. It must become the self it essentially is, or it never becomes a self at all. If this necessary self, this essential self, is forgotten in preoccupation with the infinite possibilities of selfhood, the self evaporates into abstract possibility.

Possibility then appears to the self ever greater and greater, more and more things become possible, because nothing becomes actual. At last it is as if everything were possible—but this is precisely when the abyss has swallowed up the self. [*SuD*, 169]

In such a case we may say the self has lost touch with reality, or, to use Kierkegaard's term, "actuality." In a sense this is true. But more basically what has been lost is necessity, for, as we have seen, actuality is a synthesis of possibility and necessity. "What really is lacking is the power to obey, to submit to the necessary in oneself, to what may be called one's limit" (*SuD*, 169).

On the other hand, one can lose himself through the loss of possibility. If possibility is not added to necessity, the self remains in despair. Unless possibility is added to the abstract essence of selfhood, the self will never be realized. "The determinist or the fatalist is in despair, and in despair he has lost his self, because for him everything is necessary" (*SuD*, 173). The determinist may well know that the necessary essence of selfhood is a synthesis of the finite and the infinite, but unless he also knows that this synthesis is sustained in freedom, his necessary essence will never become actual.

And possibility is not just probability. The Philistine, like the fatalist, has lost his grasp on possibility. But whereas the fatalist has enough imagination to grasp the necessity of selfhood, though not enough to grasp its possibility, the Philistine has not enough imagination for either. He exists neither on the plane of possibility nor on that of necessity, but on the plane of the probable. He exists in triviality. He bases his life on what usually occurs—the probable. And if reality sometimes thrusts him into situations that transcend this trivial wisdom, he learns of his despair. But to become a self, "imagination must enable a man to soar higher than the misty precinct of the probable" (*SuD*, 174).

Kierkegaard likens freedom, or possibility, to the breath of life itself. Without possibility the self will suffocate.

> Personality is a synthesis of possibility and necessity. The condition of its survival is therefore analogous to breathing (respiration), which is an in- and an a-spiration. The self of the determinist cannot breathe, for it is impossible to breathe necessity alone, which taken pure and simple suffocates the human self. [*SuD*, 173]

Here, as in the discussion of finitude-infinitude, Kierkegaard introduces the theological dimension. In the wordplay of the above quotation, Spirit is acknowledged as the fundamental Power of being. The dialectic of selfhood is an in-spiration and an a-spiration. This spiritual dialectic, which is analogous to breathing, constitutes Kierkegaard's understanding of prayer.

To pray is to breathe, and possibility is for the self what

oxygen is for breathing. But . . . in order to pray there
must be a God, there must be a self plus possibility, or a
self and possibility in the pregnant sense; for God *is* that
all things are possible, and that all things are possible *is*
God. . . . The fact that God's will is the possible makes it
possible for me to pray; if God's will is only the necessary,
man is essentially as speechless as the brutes. [*SuD*,
173-74]

This is to say, if ultimately reality is the necessary, selfhood is
impossible; selfhood is possible only if ultimately freedom is
real. "The fatalist is in despair—he has lost God, and therefore
himself as well; for if he has not God, neither has he a self. But
the fatalist has no God—or, what is the same thing, his god is
necessity" (*SuD*, 173).

Kierkegaard is clear about the ontological status of freedom.
Freedom, or possibility, is not self-willed. Precisely at the moment "when a man is brought to the utmost extremity, so that
humanly speaking no possibility exists" (*SuD*, 171), the decisive question is put: whether, nevertheless, possibility appears.
Kierkegaard observes that "sometimes the inventiveness of
human imagination suffices to procure possibility, but in the
last resort . . . the only help is this, that for God all things are
possible" (*SuD*, 172). God is the possibility that comes to man
even when his imagination can no longer conjure up a possibility. And then the question is whether man will *believe*,
whether he will appropriate this possibility as his own possibility.

Kierkegaard is saying that God *is* possibility—genuine, ontological possibility—that freedom, or Spirit, is ontologically
real. The next question is that of the reality of the self. What is
the norm of selfhood? And what is the ontological status of
this norm?

The Temporal and the Eternal

We have considered the dialectic of selfhood with regard to its essence and with regard to its existence. We must now undertake the final and decisive consideration—selfhood with regard to its reality. We have seen that essentially the self is a dialectical relation between the finite, immediate self one is, and the infinite image of the self which Spirit projects before it. And we have also seen that this necessary essence comes into existence only with freedom, so that existentially the self is a dialectical relation between necessity and possibility. Now we must examine the ontological reality of this dialectic. Since the self is essentially a relation which relates itself to its own self by means of its projected image of selfhood, it is evident that the reality of the self is dependent upon the reality of its transcendent norm. The importance of this transcendent norm for Kierkegaard is apparent in his study of the gradations of despair, or nonbeing. The criterion of the norm is the degree of consciousness "of having a self in which there is after all something eternal" (*SuD,* 210). Thus, considered under the aspect of reality, the self is a dialectical relation between the temporal and the eternal.

Based on this criterion, Kierkegaard distinguishes three stages in the emergence of the self. Or, since the self may content itself with existence on any one of these planes, they may be called three modes of selfhood. These are the aesthetic, the ethical, and the religious modes of being, or, as I shall designate them, the aesthetic self, the ethical self, and the theological self. Which mode of being will prevail depends upon the ultimate referent of the self. For the aesthetic self, *pathos* or feeling is the test of truth; for the ethical self, *ethos* or the relative value system of one's society is the norm; and for the theological self, *theos* or Spirit is the ultimate referent. It is the last of these, of course, which Kierkegaard calls "the eternal." The individual may be vaguely conscious of the eternal in his aesthetic mode of being, or he may be more acutely conscious of the eternal in the ethical mode of being, but he is only fully conscious of the eternal in the religious mode of being.

Without a consciousness of the eternal dimension, the individual exists solely on the temporal plane.

> The sensuous nature and the psycho-sensuous completely dominate him; . . . he lives in the sensuous categories agreeable/disagreeable, and says goodbye to truth etc.; . . . he is too sensuous to have the courage to venture to be spirit or to endure it. [*SuD*, 176]

Or, as Kierkegaard expresses it later,

> The *immediate* man (in so far as immediacy is to be found without any reflection) is merely soulishly determined, his self or he himself is a something included along with the other in the compass of the temporal and the worldly, and it has only an illusory appearance of possessing in it something eternal. [*SuD*, 184]

Such an immediate man is not really a self. He is in despair, for despair is the loss of the eternal, and the eternal is what he does not have. He has his being in things. When he is deprived of things, when something "happens" to deprive him of them, he thinks he is in despair. But actually he was already in despair for he lacked the eternal.

Of course there is probably no one who is wholly without self-reflection. Suppose, then, that this immediate man does have some self-reflection, some sense of a transcendent or eternal self, and yet does not become a self. Such a man, by means of self-reflection,

> has an obscure conception that there may even be something eternal in the self. But in vain he struggles thus; the difficulty he stumbled against demands a breach with immediacy as a whole, and for that he has not sufficient self-reflection or ethical reflection. [*SuD*, 188]

There is yet another refinement to this aesthetic level of existence. First there is the immediate man who is wholly unaware of the eternal dimension of selfhood. Such a man has his being in things and despairs over the loss of things. Then there is the immediate man in whom there is some self-reflection. This man is vaguely aware that there may be an eternal referent for the self but is too weak to break with immediacy, i.e. to break with having his being in things, in the temporal. Such a man's despair is the despair of weakness. Now Kierkegaard suggests that there is an intensification of this despair when this man is self-consciously in despair over his weakness. In every case, however, the man remains an "aesthetic self" whose frame of reference is his *pathos* or desires. He has his existence solely in the temporal.

Finally, there is the man who, in an awareness of the eternal and of his own impotence, defiantly wills to be a self. Here the ethical mode of being comes into full flower. Not only is this man conscious of his weakness and of a transcendent dimension of the self, but he is also conscious of the reason why he does not want to be a self. He knows that he is not willing to find his selfhood by losing himself. His response is Stoic courage. He defiantly wills to be a self, but the self as he himself defines it. As Kierkegaard expresses it:

> In order to will in despair to be oneself there must be consciousness of the infinite self. This infinite self, however, is really only the abstractest form, the abstractest possibility of the self, and it is this self the man despairingly wills to be, detaching the self from every relation to the Power which posited it, or detaching it from the conception that there is such a Power in existence. By the aid of this infinite form the self despairingly wills to dispose of itself or to create itself, to make itself the self it wills to be. [*SuD*, 201]

Such an existence is not without a high degree of consciousness of the eternal dimension of human existence, but it is still despair—the despair of defiance for the self defiantly determines its own transcendent norm. Kierkegaard charges that there is no ontological seriousness here. "It [this self] acknowledges no power over it, hence in the last resort it lacks seriousness"; it lacks the idea "that God is regarding one, instead of which the despairing self is content with regarding itself" (*SuD*, 202). He adds,

> It is so far from being true that the self succeeds more and more in becoming itself, that in fact it merely becomes more and more manifest that it is a hypothetical self. . . . The self wants to enjoy the entire satisfaction of making itself into itself, of developing itself, of being itself. [*SuD*, 203]

But this is sheer subjectivism. There is no ontological reality to such a self. It is simply an arbitrary, subjective ideal or at best an ideal image of selfhood acquired from the parents or from culture. Such a person is an "ethical self" whose frame of reference is the *ethos* of his culture.

Kierkegaard is not content with this purely relative image of selfhood. "The child who hitherto has had only the parents to measure himself by, becomes a self when he is a man by getting the state as a measure. But what an infinite accent falls upon the self by getting God as a measure!" (*SuD*, 210). Thus he now adds a theological dimension to his interpretation of the dialectic of selfhood. As he puts it:

> The gradations in the consciousness of the self with which we have hitherto been employed are within the definition of the human self, or the self whose measure is man. But this self acquires a new quality or qualification in the fact that it is the self directly in the sight of God. This self is no longer the merely human self but is what I would call . . . the theological self, the self directly in the sight of God. And what an infinite reality this self acquires by being before God! [*SuD*, 210]

Such a person Kierkegaard calls the "theological self" whose ultimate referent is Spirit, the eternal *theos*. It should be apparent that this transcendent referent of selfhood is no mere subjective projection, nor even a cultural image of man. The eternal Spirit, in relation to which we have our existence, is ontologically real. Consequently, despair is not merely an ethical concept but a theological one. Sin is not just the violation of a relationship to an ethical ideal, it is the violation of the God-relationship—not a violation of the *ethos*, but of the *theos*.

The self is given with its existence the task of relating its temporal self to the eternal, and then it supplants the eternal with something temporal. The difference between the temporal and the eternal is qualitatively infinite; "God and man are two qualities between which there is an infinite qualitative difference" (*SuD*, 257). To relate oneself to some self-determined norm of selfhood is not to be related to the eternal, but simply to the temporal. "The pagan and the natural man have as their measure the merely human self" (*SuD*, 211), whereas Christianity insists that man exists "before God." This is the offensive thing about Christianity. It makes *God* the measure, and that is asking too much. So men cut the measure down to size thereby reducing the stature of the self. Kierkegaard says,

> A self is qualitatively what its measure is. That Christ is the measure is on God's part attested as the expression for the immense reality a self possesses; for it is true for the first time in Christ that God is man's goal and measure. [*SuD*, 244-45]

This is to say that in Jesus Christ the relation between the temporal and the eternal was consummated, that in Jesus Christ for the first time it really came about that God was a man's goal and measure. Hence, Jesus Christ is the paradigm of selfhood; in him the temporal and the eternal meet. In this historical person the reality of the self is infinitely potentiated by receiving God as its measure, by existing before God. So, when one exists in Christ's mode of being, his reality is infinitely potentiated, for he has become a self. As Kierkegaard summarizes:

First there came ... ignorance of having an eternal self;
then knowledge of having a self wherein there is after all
something eternal. Thereupon ... it was shown that this
distinction is referable to the self which has a human conception of itself or whose goal is man. The contrast to this
was a self face to face with God, and this was taken as the
basis of the definition of sin. Now comes a self face to face
with Christ. [*SuD*, 244]

2. Freud's Concept of the Ego

Libido: The Power of Selfhood

The problem of stating Freud's concept of the self is complicated by the fact that his theory was in a continual state of flux. In contrast to Kierkegaard, who wrote all his major works in slightly more than a single decade, Freud's writings span almost half a century. Whereas Kierkegaard's concepts possess a certain constancy, Freud was continually modifying his conceptual formulations, giving new definition to old terminology in an exasperatingly fluid way. Consequently, his thought must be treated historically, as constantly evolving theory rather then a fixed body of dogma.

The development is not without direction, however. It proceeds from the somatic to the psychological to the "metapsychological," as Freud termed it.[1] In his early period, which was characterized by somatic reduction, a dualistic interpretation was postulated in which the self was understood as a function of the organism's physical drives, the sex-instinct and the ego-instinct. In his psychological period the dichotomy was transformed into two manifestations of a single psychic

---

1. B. H. Stoodley has done a detailed study of this threefold development of Freud's theory in *The Concepts of Sigmund Freud* (Glencoe, Ill.: The Free Press, 1959). He notes the transition in Freud's theory from a biological to a psychological to a social interpretation of the self. I prefer to employ Freud's own term *metapsychological* for the last phase, however, inasmuch as it connotes a certain metaphysical dimension, which Freud intended.

energy, object-libido and ego-libido. And in his metapsychological period the Libido concept evolved into Eros, the life-
instinct, in tension with Thanatos, the death-instinct.

The somatic element was fully recognized by Freud in his
early attempts to formulate a comprehensive theory of the
self. Indeed, in this period of his work it was the sole explana-
tory principle. He sought to explain the phenomena of selfhood by means of an "instinct theory." His earliest formulation of this theory defined an instinct as "the psychic repre-
sentation of a continually flowing inner somatic source of
stimulation." He added,

> What distinguishes the instincts from one another . . . is
> their relation to their somatic sources and to their aims.
> The source of the instinct is an exciting process in an
> organ, and the immediate aim of the instinct lies in the
> release of this organic stimulus. [*TCTS,* 576]

On this basis he distinguished two basic instincts: the drive for
the preservation of the individual, or the ego-instinct, whose
psychic representative is hunger; and the drive for the preservation of the species, or the sex-instinct, whose psychic representative is Libido. Both drives are somatic in origin and have
their own peculiar kind of energy system associated with
them. The ego-instinct originates in the digestive organs and
finds its gratification in eating. The sex-instinct originates in
the reproductive organs and finds its gratification in the sexual
act.

Freud never fully developed his ego-instinct theory, but he
spent years perfecting his sexual-instinct theory and applying
it to the vicissitudes of the self. Borrowing a concept from the
physics of his day, he postulated that the various psychoneuroses could be made intelligible by means of Libido, a
somatic energy analogous to an electric current:

> I should like finally to dwell for a moment on the hypoth-
> esis which I have made use of in the exposition of the

defence neuroses. I mean the conception that among the psychic functions there is something which should be differentiated (an amount of affect, a sum of excitation), something having all the attributes of a quantity—although we possess no means of measuring it—a something which is capable of increase, decrease, displacement and discharge, and which extends itself over the memory-traces of an idea like an electric charge over the surface of the body. We can apply this hypothesis . . . in the same sense as the physicist employs the conception of a fluid electric current. [*CP*, I, 75]

This energy is somatic in origin and sexual in character. It originates from the excitation of the sexual organs and normally is discharged in the sexual act. The psychoneuroses, it was postulated, occur when this normal process is frustrated. In such a case, the Libido is dammed up and finds no adequate outlet. In hysteria the Libido finds an outlet in abnormal, substitutive, physical manifestations. In the obsessional neuroses it is invested in substitutive ideas. And in anxiety neuroses the Libido finds no outlet whatever, thereby creating a state of suspense or anxiety (*CP*, I, 61-74). The somatic and sexual character of this energy concept is made quite explicit in the following quotation:

From all these data: that an accumulation of excitation is involved; that the anxiety which probably represents this accumulated excitation is of somatic origin, so that it is somatic excitation which is accumulated; further, that the somatic excitation is of a sexual nature and that a decline in the psychical share in the sexual process goes along with it—all these data prepare our minds for the statement that the mechanism of anxiety-neurosis is to be sought in the deflection of somatic sexual excitation from the psychical field, and in an abnormal use of it, due to this deflection. [*CP*, I, 97]

Thus, in this first phase of theoretical development Libido is conceived to be a quantum of energy, somatic in origin and sexual in quality. While Freud was convinced there was a corresponding energy concept associated with the ego-instincts, he never developed it to any degree.

In the second phase of his theoretical work, when he turned his attention more and more to the psychic component of the sexual-instinct, Freud introduced a modification in his use of the term *sexual*. Earlier, Libido was understood to be derived explicitly from the sex organs; here he says, "This sexual excitement is furnished not only from the so-called sexual parts alone, but from all organs of the body" (*TCTS,* 611). This greatly extended the meaning of the word *sexual* with regard to the origin of Libido. Later he also broadened its use with regard to its aim:

> We reckon as belonging to 'sexual life' all expressions of tender feeling, which spring from the source of primitive sexual feelings, even when those feelings have become inhibited in regard to their original sexual aim or have exchanged this aim for another which is no longer sexual.
> [*CP,* II, 299]

While Freud never fully developed his ego-instinct theory, his treatment of the transmutation of the libidinal aim presupposes an ego which may become the object of the libidinal drives, and a reservoir of libidinal energy from which this energy may be dispensed and directed. Libido thus invested he designates as narcissistic or *ego-libido,* in contrast to its more immediate manifestation which he calls *object-libido.* He says, "The narcissistic or ego-libido appears to us as the great reservoir from which all object cathexis is sent out, and into which it is drawn back again." Once invested in an object, this object-libido "may be withdrawn from the object, . . . preserved in a floating state in special states of tension, and . . . it may finally be taken back into the ego and again changed into ego-libido as *narcissistic libido* (*TCTS,* 611).

Here Freud has introduced a notion which essentially under-
mines his distinction between the ego-instinct and the sexual-
instinct. These are virtually reduced to two manifestations of a
common power, Libido. Although the implications of this reduction were not accepted by him for some time, he was not
oblivious to the threat which this development posed to his
doctrine of the two instincts. For example, he asked rhetori-
cally:

> If we concede to the ego a primary cathexis of libido, why
> is there any necessity for further distinguishing a sexual
> libido from a nonsexual energy pertaining to the ego-
> instincts? Would not the assumption of a uniform mental
> energy save us all the difficulties of differentiating the
> energy of the ego-instincts from ego-libido, and ego-libido
> from object-libido? [*CP*, IV, 33-34]

But, defending the validity of the distinction, he declared, "It
is impossible to suppose that a unity comparable to the ego
can exist in the individual from the very start; the ego has to
develop" (*CP*, IV, 34). Auto-erotic behavior is one of the earliest manifestations of sexual energy, however, and there must
be another instinct operative here—the drive toward selfhood
or the ego-instinct. Actually, it was not until 1920, in *Beyond
the Pleasure Principle*, that Freud was able to admit the collapse of his dualistic instinct theory. But what he removed
with the one hand, he restored with the other. The somatic
dualism was transmuted into a psychic dualism in which the
various phenomena of selfhood were interpreted as a function
of the Libido in both its narcissistic and objective forms. He
summarized this evolution of his Libido concept:

> Libido which was . . . lodged in the ego was described as
> 'narcissistic'. This narcissistic libido was of course also a
> manifestation of the force of the sexual instinct in the
> analytical sense of those words, and it had necessarily to
> be identified with the 'self-preservative instincts' whose

existence had been recognized from the first. Thus the original opposition between the ego instincts and the sexual instincts proved to be inadequate. A portion of the ego instincts was seen to be libidinal; sexual instincts—probably alongside others—operated in the ego. . . . The distinction between the two kinds of instinct, which was originally regarded as in some sort of way *qualitative,* must now be characterized differently—namely as being *topographical.* [*BPP,* 91-92]

But this formulation of a psychic dualism was just a transition on the way to Freud's mature instinct theory. His metaphysical curiosity pushed him on beyond the somatic and the psychological to the metapsychological theory of the self. The principle which governs the libidinal phenomena he called the *pleasure principle.*

The mental apparatus endeavours to keep the quantity of excitation present in it as low as possible or at least to keep it constant. This latter hypothesis is only another way of stating the pleasure principle; for if the work of the mental apparatus is directed towards keeping the quantity of excitation low, then anything that is calculated to increase that quantity is bound to be felt as adverse to the functioning of the apparatus, that is as unpleasurable. [*BPP,* 24]

Of course the pleasure principle is not the sole sovereign of the mind. If this were the case all our mental processes would be pleasurable, whereas experience indicates differently. Freud suggested that the drive for pleasure jeopardizes the very existence of the organism, first, because it conflicts with the pleasure drives of other organisms and, second, because unless some consideration is given to realistic means of gratification, the energy will be dissipated in hallucination. Thus, if the organism is to survive, the pleasure principle must be modified by a regard for reality. This Freud referred to as the *reality principle*. The Libido is inhibited in its expression, in obedience to the reality principle, by means of its investment in the ego which directs its expenditure.

This Libido theory proved to be a fruitful working hypothesis. But, in the course of his clinical practice, Freud encountered a persistent phenomenon which could not be explained by the pleasure principle, even with the addition of the reality principle. This was the repetition compulsion. Freud had long noted the tendency of the repressed impulses to reassert themselves, even at the cost of unpleasure. He referred to this as the "return of the repressed." "That, however," he observed, "is unpleasure of a kind we have already considered and does not contradict the pleasure principle" (*BPP*, 42). That is, an impulse, which in the primary system aims at pleasure, has been repressed because it is a threat to the ego. Nevertheless, it still seeks to satisfy the primary aim for immediate gratification. This return of the repressed, therefore, simultaneously represents the drive for pleasure in the primary system and the experience of unpleasure in the ego.

Now, however, Freud encountered a different aspect of this repetition compulsion—the compulsion to repeat a past experience which entailed no pleasure whatever even for the primary system. Such a compulsion sometimes completely dominates a person's life, giving "the appearance of some 'daemonic' force at work" (*BPP*, 65). The individual continually reenacts a painful situation of the past. Enough is left unexplained by the pleasure principle, even with the addition of the reality principle, to warrant the assumption of another drive "more primitive, more elementary, more instinctual than the pleasure principle which it over-rides" (*BPP*, 46-47). This is the *"urge inherent in organic life to restore an earlier state of things* which the living entity has been obliged to abandon under the pressure of external disturbing forces" (*BPP*, 67). To sustain this thesis Freud employed an evolutionary theory.

> The attributes of life were at some time evoked in inanimate matter by the action of a force of whose nature we can form no conception. . . . The tension which then arose in what had hitherto been inanimate substance endeavoured to cancel itself out. In this way the first instinct came into being: the instinct to return to the inanimate state. [*BPP*, 71]

The function of the Libido is to perpetuate the organism's existence in spite of its pursuit of the instinctual path toward death. In this manner, Freud had again modified his dualistic understanding of the self. The metapsychological dualism of the life-instinct and the death-instinct supplanted the psychological dualism of object-libido and ego-libido.

In his discussion of this new instinct theory, Freud found the term *sexual instinct* too limited to denote the reality with which he was dealing. We have seen how he had continually found it necessary to broaden the meaning of the term *sexual.* Eventually, in *Beyond the Pleasure Principle,* he found that the term had been stretched beyond its limit. He supplanted it with the more comprehensive concept, *Eros.* Freud summarized this development:

> We came to know what the 'sexual instincts' were from their relation to the sexes and to the reproductive function. We retained this name after we had been obliged by the findings of psychoanalysis to connect them less closely with reproduction. With the hypothesis of narcissistic libido and the extension of the concept of libido to the individual cells, the sexual instinct was transformed for us into Eros. . . . What are commonly called the sexual instincts are looked upon by us as the part of Eros which is directed towards objects. Our speculations have suggested that Eros operates from the beginning of life and appears as a 'life instinct' in opposition to the 'death instinct' which was brought into being by the coming to life of inorganic substance. These speculations seek to solve the

riddle of life by supposing that these two instincts were struggling with each other from the very first. [*BPP*, 105-06 n.]

With this formulation, the concept of Libido has made the full transition from a somatic concept to a psychological concept to a metapsychological concept. And the early somatic dualism has evolved into a metapsychological dualism of Eros and Thanatos. Eros is the fundamental power of being which continually resists the somatic inertia of nonbeing or Thanatos.[2] The psychological element is retained in the fact that Eros first manifests itself in the basic life drives (e.g., sex and hunger) which are primitive forms of the drive for selfhood, or the ego-instinct. And the somatic element is preserved in the tendency to return to the inorganic state of quiescence.

The Ego and the Id

Whatever else may be said of Freud's understanding of the self, it is essentially dualistic in character. Though his clinical observations continually required him to revise his conception of the nature of this dualism, he never abandoned the fundamental conviction that man is to be understood dualistically. We have seen that for Freud the power of being is Eros, which seeks to overcome the inertia of nonbeing or Thanatos. My concern in this section is to investigate the implications of this for a theory of the self. What is the essential structure of the self? How does the self come into being? And what constitutes its reality?

Again, due to the evolutionary character of Freud's theories, I will approach these questions historically and will note that the progression of his studies is from the somatic to the psychological to the metapsychological. Freud's earliest attempt to formulate a comprehensive theory of the self, in *The Interpretation of Dreams* (1900), set forth a mechanical model of

2. Herbert Marcuse arrives at the same conclusion in *Eros and Civilization* (New York: Alfred A. Knopf, Vintage Books, 1962), p. 113.

the structure of selfhood. But his increasing awareness of the
historical dimension of the self forced him to greatly modify
this early theory. This development culminated in *The Ego
and the Id* in 1923. Significantly, Freud's understanding of
"reality" underwent a similar development from "material
reality" to "social reality" to a search for some trans-social
reality. But the fundamental understanding of the self as a
relation which relates itself to reality was consistently maintained.

In *The Interpretation of Dreams* Freud set forth his first
theory of the self. He distinguished between "primary processes" and "secondary processes," between the "first ψ-
system" which is given by nature and the "second ψ-system"
which develops historically. The first ψ-system is immediately
given with human existence. It would not be accurate to call
this organic energy system a "self," though later Freud did
refer to it as the "pleasure-ego." It is a purely instinctual organism in this primal state. Any unfulfilled organic need
creates a state of inner tension experienced as a desire or wish.
Or, put in terms of Freud's Libido theory, the unfulfilled need
is the source of libidinal energy, the accumulation of which is
felt as pain and the release of which is perceived as pleasure.
"Such a current in the apparatus, issuing from pain and striving for pleasure we call a wish" (*IoD,* 533). This is what he
later called the pleasure/pain principle which governs the operation of the primary ψ-system. Technically, the wish is the
psychological component of the somatic need or instinct.
Freud notes, "An instinct can never be an object of consciousness—only the idea that represents the instinct" (*CP,* IV,
109), i.e. the wish.

> The first occurrence of wishing may well have taken the
> form of a hallucinatory cathexis of the memory gratifica-
> tion. But this hallucination, unless it could be maintained
> to the point of exhaustion, proved incapable of bringing
> about a cessation of the need, and consequently of se-

curing the pleasure connected with gratification. [*IoD*, 533]

Unless a second mental process is imposed upon this wishful activity it will result in no real gratification. The self would dissipate in hallucination.

The secondary ψ-system must perform an inhibitory function. Whereas "the activity of the first ψ-system aims at *the free outflow of the quantities of excitation,*" the second ψ-system "effects an inhibition of this outflow" (*IoD*, 534). It must inhibit the expenditure of energy in hallucinatory activity in order that this energy may be employed in realistic activity to obtain the desired object. In effect, the primary processes image the possibilities of gratification, while the secondary processes inhibit the complete investment of energy in such hallucinatory activity so that some particular possibility may be realized. This secondary development is essential if the organism is to survive. Some kind of restraining mechanism is necessary to enable the organism to tolerate temporary displeasure for the sake of real, though delayed, gratification.

This secondary ψ-system constitutes the "reality-ego" in contrast with the primary ψ-system or "pleasure-ego." Where the latter is given by nature, so to speak, the former comes into being historically.

> The primary processes are present in the apparatus from the beginning, while the secondary processes only take shape gradually during the course of life, inhibiting and overlaying the primary, whilst gaining complete control over them perhaps only in the prime of life. Owing to this belated arrival of the secondary processes, the essence of our being, consisting of unconscious wish-impulses, remains something which cannot be grasped or inhibited by the pre-conscious; and its part is once and for all restricted to indicating the most appropriate paths for the wish-impulses originating in the unconscious. [*IoD*, 536]

Thus the self comes into being as a necessary functional structure which relates the primary unconscious drives to realistic
objects of gratification.

In the above quotation Freud refers to the unconscious
wish-impulses as the essence of our being. He elaborates:

> The unconscious is the true psychic reality; in its inner
> nature it is just as much unknown to us as the reality of
> the external world, and it is just as imperfectly communi-
> cated to us by the data of consciousness as is the external
> world by the reports of our sense-organs. [*IoD*, 542]

Freud tried to get behind the phenomenal self to its inner
reality through a study of the dream processes. This study was
mainly concerned with the relation of the self to its psychic
reality. However, he warned that "psychic reality is a special
form of existence which must not be confounded with material reality" (*IoD*, 548). And, as we have seen, the self is a
relation between this psychic reality and material reality. If
the relation to external reality is not sustained, the self may be
lost in hallucination.

When Freud picked up this theme in his essay, "Two Principles of Mental Functioning" (1911), he directed his attention to the relation of the self to external reality thus "bring-
ing the psychological significance of the real outer world into
the structure of our theory" (*CP*, IV, 13). He summarized the
argument presented in *The Interpretation of Dreams:*

> The state of mental equilibrium was originally disturbed
> by the peremptory demands of inner needs. . . . Whatever
> was thought of (desired) was simply imagined in an hallu-
> cinatory form. . . . This attempt at satisfaction by means
> of hallucination was abandoned only in consequence of
> the absence of the expected gratification, because of the
> disappointment experienced. Instead the mental apparatus
> had to decide to form a conception of the real circum-
> stances in the outer world and to exert itself to alter them.

A new principle of mental functioning was thus introduced; what was conceived of was no longer that which
was pleasant, but that which was real, even if it should be
unpleasant. This institution of the *reality-principle* proved
a momentous step. [*CP*, IV, 14]

As Freud put it elsewhere, "The transition from the pleasure-
principle to the reality-principle is one of the most important
advances in the development of the ego" (*GIP*, 365). Actually,
the transition to the reality principle does not mean the oblit-
eration of the pleasure principle; it simply assures the pleasure-ego's realistic gratification. The function of the reality-ego
is not to supplant the pleasure-ego, in the sense that the primal
drives are annulled, but to relate the pleasure-ego to external
reality. Therefore, the essential function of the secondary ψ-
system (the ego) is to sustain a satisfactory relation between
the wishful possibilities of the primary ψ-system (the id) and
the necessities of external reality.

The Ego and the Superego

As we have seen, the essential structure of the self is functional
in character. The self is essentially a functional mechanism
which relates the libidinal drive to reality. It does not exist in
the primal situation but comes into being historically. But the
question persists concerning how the historical self comes into
being. The description of selfhood set forth above is basically a
somatic reduction limited to the categories of nature. Increasingly Freud turned his attention to the historical dimension of
selfhood. In his study of narcissism, published in 1914, he
took up the problem of how the essential self comes into
existence.

It has been noted that the spontaneous desires of the pleasure-ego must be inhibited or the self is lost in hallucination.
But how is this inhibition accomplished? Freud observes,

The very impressions, experiences, impulses and desires

that one man indulges . . . will be rejected with the utmost indignation by another, or stifled at once even before they enter consciousness. The difference between the two, however . . . can easily be expressed in terms of the libido-theory. We may say that the one man has set up an *ideal* in himself by which he measures his actual ego, while the other is without this formation of an ideal. [*CP*, IV, 50-51]

It is the projection of this ideal-ego which makes possible the inhibition of the Libido. Freud adds, "That which he projects ahead of him as his ideal is merely his substitute for the lost narcissism of his childhood—the time when he was his own ideal" (*CP*, IV, 51). Thus, the inhibition of the Libido is accomplished through a shift in its cathexis from the reality-ego to the ideal-ego, which then determines which modes of expenditure will be permitted. The ideal-ego, therefore, is an effective instrument for inhibiting the Libido.

There are two ways in which the Libido may be inhibited, through repression or through sublimation. Repression involves the denial of the libidinal impulses, whereas sublimation channels the libidinal energy into acceptable modes of expression. The latter is ultimately the only satisfactory method. Inhibition does not really permit expression of the libidinal energy but simply dams it up. And this, as we shall see, leads to a sickness or distortion of the self. While sublimation may be indicated by the ideal-ego, it is not thereby necessitated. "It is true that the ideal-ego requires such sublimation, but it cannot enforce it; sublimation remains a special process which may be prompted by the ideal but the execution of which is entirely independent of any such incitement" (*CP*, IV, 52). This function remains with the reality-ego.

But what is it that causes the reality-ego to project such an ideal? Freud wrote:

That which prompted the person to form an ego-ideal, over which his conscience keeps guard, was the influence of parental criticism . . . , reinforced, as time went on, by those who trained and taught the child and by all the other persons of his environment—an indefinite host, too numerous to reckon (fellow-men, public opinion). [*CP,* IV, 52]

The process which establishes the ideal-ego was developed at length in *Group Psychology and the Analysis of the Ego* (1921). The central notion is *identification.* "Identification is known to psychoanalysis as the earliest expression of an emotional tie with another person" (*GP&AE,* 46). At first the child's Libido is entirely invested in himself; it is "autoerotic." Then the boy begins to show a special interest in his father. He identifies himself with his father. That is, he adopts an identity by taking his father as his ideal. This is the first step in the evolution of the ideal-ego.

Later, a libidinal interest in his mother develops. For a period, these two distinct emotional ties exist side by side. Gradually they merge and what Freud called the *Oedipus complex* results from their confluence. The mother becomes the object of the libidinal interest, but the father, whom the child has taken as his own ideal, constitutes his rival. Consequently, an ambivalent attitude toward the father develops. The child both loves and hates him. He identifies with him and yet resents his competition for the mother's love. In normal development the identification wins out. "This first configuration of the child's love, which in typical cases takes the shape of the Oedipus complex, succumbs . . . to a wave of repression" (*GP&AE,* 90). Due to the strong bonds of identification with the father, the child's ego sanctions what he sanctions and forbids what he forbids. This period is known as the period of latency, "during which ethical restraints are built up to act as defences against the desires of the Oedipus complex" (*CP,* V, 120).

The original ego ideal which was formed by identification with the father is augmented by all the countless, though much less significant, relationships the child has with other people. "Each individual is a component part of numerous groups, he is bound by ties of identification in many directions, and he has built up his ideal upon the various models" (*GP&AE,* 78). It is this composite ego ideal which, through its censoring activity, enables the reality-ego to repress the Oedipus desires. In short, the ego becomes divided against itself. "The ego now enters into the relation of an object to the ego ideal which developed out of it," although "in many individuals the separation between the ego and the ego ideal is not very far advanced" (*GP&AE,* 79).

In due time, when the ego ideal has become internalized or "introjected," to use Freud's term, and the necessary ethical restraints have been built up, the latent libidinal drives revive and seek an external object once again, but this time under the control of the reality-ego which seeks to assure a realistic means of gratification. This period of libidinal reawakening is apparent at puberty. In addition to choosing a realistic object of libidinal interest, the reality-ego is able to divert a portion of the libidinal energy into other forms of activity. This is the function called "sublimation," to which I have previously referred. In the creation of community such aim-inhibited Libido has a great advantage over that which is uninhibited. Since the sublimated Libido is not capable of complete satisfaction, it is especially effective in creating permanent communal ties which continually strain toward gratification precisely because they are never fully satisfied.

In summary, the self begins as an organism whose behavior is dominated by instinctual impulses. In order to survive it must find a way to inhibit this libidinal expenditure and to channel it into realistic paths of gratification. This it accomplishes by investing the Libido in the reality-ego which directs its expenditure. But within a particular cultural context certain modes of gratification are not permitted. The necessary libidinal inhibition and sublimation are accomplished with the aid of a projected ego ideal which functions as a censor. The energy which was originally invested in the reality-ego is now invested in the ideal-ego and expended in accordance with the ego ideal. Thus the self is understood to be a relation between the libidinal desires of the pleasure-ego and the transcendent norms of the ideal-ego. The stability of this new constellation is constantly threatened. The unconscious, repressed portion of the self continually threatens to destroy the relationship, and, as Freud observes, "It is quite conceivable that the separation of the ego ideal from the ego cannot be borne for long either" (*GP&AE,* 81). In short, the self must continually posit the relationship if it is to remain a self.

This study of the dynamics of becoming a self culminated in the little book, *The Ego and the Id* (1923). Here Freud introduced a more precise terminology for the various processes involved in the self—the terminology which has become identified with psychoanalysis. He dropped the term *pleasure-ego* and called the primal human entity the *id (das Es),* for the apparent reason that at this stage man is not yet a self but an "it." He reserved the term *ego (das Ich)* for the *reality-ego,* the process whereby the self relates itself to external reality. "The ego is that part of the id which has been modified by the direct influence of the external world" (*E&I,* 29). Finally, he noted that the ego is not merely that modification of the id which is effected by interaction with its physical environment, it also undergoes a second modification in its relation to its social environment. The *ideal-ego* which results, he now terms the *superego (das Überich)* which performs a normative function in the dialectic of selfhood. The considerations which led to the assumption of a differentiating grade within the ego have already been set forth. Thus, to paraphrase Kierkegaard's definition of the self, the ego is a relation which relates the id to the superego.

The Notion of Reality

We have seen that the id is essentially an immediate relation between the somatic and the psychic elements of the self and that the ego is a mediate relation—a relation which relates the id to reality. But Freud's understanding of *reality* has not been made explicit. He employed the term in many ways, but again the movement of his thought was from the somatic to the psychological to the metapsychological, or from material reality to psychic reality to social ideality.

Freud consistently referred to "psychic reality," rather than "material reality," as the essence of selfhood, though the self cannot exist without a relation to the latter. He repeatedly referred to the Libido as "the essence of our being," the "true psychic reality," and so forth (*IoD*, 536, 542). Thus, the primal reality of the self is Libido. Libido is its fundamental power of selfhood. In its primitive state the "self" is basically a bundle of drives, "a chaos, a cauldron of seething excitement" (*NIL*, 104-05). But such a "self" is not yet a self, as Freud indicated by the designation he gave it. This mode of "selfhood" he called an *it* or the *id*. In the id mode of being, reality is defined by the desires of the it. The pleasure principle is determinative. The id exists in the categories pleasure/unpleasure *(Lust/Unlust)*.

Freud was aware of the problems involved in positing a mode of existence totally determined by the pleasure principle. In a footnote to his essay on "Two Principles in Mental Functioning" he wrote:

> It will rightly be objected that an organization which is a slave to the pleasure-principle and neglects the reality of the outer world could not maintain itself alive for the shortest time, so that it could not have come into being at all. The use of a fiction of this kind is, however, vindicated by the consideration that the infant . . . does almost realize such a state of mental life. Probably it hallucinates the fulfilment of its inner needs; it betrays its 'pain' due to increase of stimulation and delay of satisfaction by the motor discharge of crying and struggling and then experiences the hallucinated satisfaction. Later, as a child, it

learns to employ intentionally these modes of discharge as means of expression. [*CP,* IV, 14-15]

And again in *The Interpretation of Dreams* he noted,

So far as we know, a psychic apparatus possessing only the primary process does not exist, and is to that extent a theoretical fiction; but this at least is a fact: that the primary processes are present in the apparatus from the beginning, while the secondary processes only take shape gradually during the course of life. [*IoD,* 536]

From this can be concluded that the id with its psychic reality has at least logical, if not temporal, priority in the dialectic of the self, and that this dimension of reality is determinative in its initial mode of existence.

As I have already indicated, however, the organism cannot even survive unless its fundamental life-drives are related to real objects of gratification. Indeed, the ego comes into existence as a relation which relates the id to external reality. For this reason the ego is referred to as a "reality-ego," in contrast to the "pleasure-ego" or the id. Here "reality" refers to material reality or realistic objects of gratification. With the development of this relationship a viable mode of selfhood has emerged, and Freud rightly reserved the term *ego* for this level in the development of the self. This mode of being is one for which material objects constitute reality. In a sense, one can say that the reality principle has replaced the pleasure principle as the determinative principle of selfhood, but actually the reality principle has simply modified the pleasure principle to assure its gratification, and such a self still exists in the categories pleasure/unpleasure.

But this does not exhaust Freud's understanding of reality. Since an important part of the context in which an individual finds himself is his culture, this cultural nexus also constitutes a dimension of reality. Freud increasingly took this into account in his evolving theory of the self. The significance of the social norm was noted as early as 1914 when Freud acknowledged the importance of an ego ideal in the development of the self (*CP*, IV, 50ff.). He elaborated on this concept in *Group Psychology and the Analysis of the Ego* (1921) and formally incorporated it into his mature theory of the self as the *superego*. Just as the ego is the functional precipitate of the encounter of the id with its material environment, so the superego is the functional precipitate of the interaction of the ego with its social environment. Although the ego is predominantly derived from the identification of the individual with his parents, it includes elements from every social grouping with which he identifies—his race, his economic class, his religion, his nationality, and so forth. The ego ideal has the force of a categorical imperative because it is a part of the essential structure of the self (*E&I*, 45).

The institution of this structure inaugurates the ethical mode of existence. By means of it, the self assumes a relation to itself. There is a differentiating grade within the ego such that it has itself as its own object. This "super" ego censors the impulses of the id with reference to a reality which transcends material reality, a reality which is really an ideality. The tension between the id which obeys the pleasure principle, and the superego which obeys an ideality principle is experienced as guilt (*E&I*, 44-49), and the self exists in the categories of guilty/not-guilty.

In summary, while the essential structure of the self may be defined as a relation which relates its own fundamental power of being to reality, what constitutes "reality" is of crucial importance. Initially that reality is a wholly immanent psychic reality. The organism is in immediate relation with its psychic reality. As such, the "self" has not yet become a self and so is appropriately designated an id. The id functions in accordance with the pleasure principle and exists in the categories of pleasure/unpleasure. However, the organism must be related to external reality if it is to survive at all. So the concept of reality is expanded to include material reality. Genuine self-hood emerges, for a structure develops whose function it is to relate the "self" to its own self and to direct its activity toward actual gratification. This emergent structure is called the ego. The ego functions in accordance with the reality principle, seeking to assure real gratification of the instinctual drives, but it still exists basically in the categories of pleasure/unpleasure. Finally, the notion of ideality or social reality is introduced with the emergence of a new structure whose function is to relate the self to the social ideal of selfhood. This mode of being is designated the superego. The superego functions in accordance with the ideality principle and exists in the categories of guilty/not-guilty.

But Freud pushed the question of the reality of the self still further. Deeply critical of culture, he was not content to let society be the ultimate determinant of selfhood. Culture is the continual conflict between Eros and Thanatos. Eros is the basis of the family, of friendships, of all forms of community. It is the impelling stimulus in art, science, philosophy, and religion—in all forms of work and of play. But every aspect of culture is a sublimated form of Eros, an inhibited expression of Eros, a fusion of life and death.

> The meaning of the evolution of culture is no longer a riddle to us. It must present to us the struggle between Eros and Death, between the instincts of life and the instincts of destruction, as it works itself out in the human species. [*C&D*, 75]

Thus culture is the structure through which Eros, the power of being, finds expression. But when the structures require too great an inhibition, when sublimation is supplanted by renunciation, then the culture has become neurotic (*C&D*, 103). However, Freud admitted to the "egocentric predicament" of culture (if I may use the term analogically) in diagnosing its own malady.

> The diagnosis of collective neurosis . . . will be confronted
> by a specific difficulty. In the neurosis of an individual we
> can use as a starting-point the contrast presented to us
> between the patient and his environment which we assume
> to be 'normal'. No such background as this would be avail-
> able for any society similarly affected; it would have to be
> supplied in some other way. [*C&D,* 104]

Thus, within the cultural context the problem is ultimately
irresolvable. Freud stepped outside his culture for his criterion—a criterion which is characteristically dualistic. He
espoused the twin gods λόγος and 'Ανάγκη, reason and necessity. In the struggle for selfhood, it is reason which is the
decisive criterion—within the limits of necessity. "Our god
λόγος is not perhaps a very powerful one." It will realize only
those ideals which 'Ανάγκη permits, and then "only in the
incalculable future." But "in the long run nothing can with-
stand reason" (*FoI,* 97-99). Thus, for the self, the ultimate
reality is not culture but Logos. Human existence is set in the
tension between Logos and Ananke.

3. Interpolation: The Dialectic of Selfhood

The task of correlating the insights of these two students of the self must now be undertaken. I have called this endeavor an "interpolation" since it is my intention to show the relation between the two conceptions of selfhood. In a way they are polar opposites, each providing an entirely different perspective on man. Freud has approached his study from a naturalistic perspective, and Kierkegaard from an historistic perspective. I am not convinced that these interpretations are mutually exclusive, that a choice must be made between them; rather, the two studies confirm and supplement each other.

Human existence is set in a double context: the context of nature and that of history. Any attempt to interpret man exclusively from either perspective can only be a half-truth. Of course, neither Freud nor Kierkegaard is oblivious of the other dimension of human existence. Each has his understanding of the other's category. Each interprets the other's central categories in terms of his own presuppositions. This means that in the end either history is naturalized or nature is historicized. Freud is a naturalistic thinker; he seeks to interpret the phenomena of human existence under the categories of nature. Insofar as man is a creature of nature these categories serve him very well. To the degree that historical existence is grounded in nature, Freud is able to contribute immeasurably to our understanding of man. But to the degree that historical existence transcends nature, Freud's naturalistic orientation is limited. Ultimately the historical cannot be contained within the categories of nature. Historical existence is not disjunctive with nature; it arises out of nature, it is grounded in nature. But historical existence is not exhausted by nature; it transcends nature and grasps after the eternal. Kierkegaard supplies this historical perspective. Nature is real for him but not ultimate; the ultimate significance of nature is history. History is "a possibility which for nature is its whole reality" (*PF*, 62). The purpose of this interpolation is to show the differences between these two perspectives on the self, the limitations of each, and the necessity of both to provide a comprehensive understanding of the self.

This interpolation will be concerned with four major problems: (1) the question of the power of selfhood—showing the relation between Kierkegaard's doctrine of Spirit and Freud's concept of Eros; (2) the question of the structure of selfhood and the relation between Kierkegaard's concept of the self and Freud's notion of the ego; (3) the problem of becoming a self, the age-old problem of freedom and determinism as treated by the two men; and, finally (4) the problem of the reality of selfhood—the problem of the norm or ultimate referent of the self and the consequent modes of being.

The Power of Selfhood

For Kierkegaard the power of selfhood is Spirit; for Freud it is Libido. Spirit is the quest for freedom or self-determination inherent in man; Libido is discussed predominantly in terms of a sex drive or instinct. What possible relation can there be between these two seemingly disparate concepts? Spirit would appear to have nothing to do with nature. It is an entirely historical concept; it is the very essence of history. Libido, on the other hand, is an entirely natural concept; its very essence is nature. I believe that these concepts are reconcilable and that Kierkegaard and Freud themselves provide the basis of this reconciliation. I maintain that Libido is Spirit viewed from the naturalistic perspective, and that Spirit is Libido viewed from the historistic perspective. In short, the two concepts represent perspectival differences in the interpretation of the same phenomena. Moreover, Freud's perspective underwent a transition such that his Libido concept increasingly took on an historical aspect.

Spirit is the power of being or selfhood. Here *selfhood* is construed as a peculiar mode of being. It is not simply a biological concept, or even solely a psychological concept, but an ontological concept having to do with the essential mode of *human* being. Spirit, then, is the inherent power of being qua human being, and the mode of being which it posits is continually threatened with the nonbeing of despair. Despair is to the self what death is to the biological organism. Hence, Spirit is the power of being in tension with the nonbeing of despair.

Selfhood is understood to be that mode of being which is characterized by freedom. We must note, however, that for Kierkegaard freedom is not indeterminateness but self-determination. Selfhood is that mode of being which is characterized by self-determination. Consequently, Spirit as the power of selfhood is the drive toward self-determination, the instinct of the self to take responsibility for itself, the impulse to relate itself to its own self.

Spirit is present in the primal or immediate mode of being as a possibility, a potentiality which is its ultimate reality. It awakens the immediate self to the possibility of selfhood by projecting its own reality, i.e. selfhood as a possibility to be actualized, and it thereby makes possible a new mode of being.

For Freud Libido is the power of selfhood. Fundamentally understood, Libido is the sexual impulse. However, this is a very limited understanding of Freud's Libido doctrine. The original notion of Libido as sexual energy was soon modified—Freud found it too restrictive for his growing understanding of the self. The concept evolved from its narrow sexual meaning to the point where Freud found it necessary to give it a new designation, Eros. The shift in designation reveals a shift in perspective. If the self is viewed only from the perspective of nature, its power of being is seen as Libido or the sexual impulse. But, as Freud increasingly took into account the historical context of selfhood, his notion of the power of being was modified. Eros supplanted Libido as the power of human being.

Eros is the power of selfhood which continually resists the inertia of nonbeing or Thanatos. It is the life-instinct, the drive for self-preservation. It first manifests itself as an ego-instinct or a sex-instinct, the former representing the drive for the preservation of the individual, and the latter that of the species. Here self-preservation is understood biologically as physical survival. But, since the reality which threatens its existence is more than physical, the life-instinct assumes other proportions. It first calls the ego into being as a defense against physical extinction, then the superego as a defense against social extinction. Eros, therefore, is truly the power of being in continual tension with Thanatos, the tendency toward nonbeing.

So construed, Eros and Spirit are not as different as it first appears. Each represents an inherent drive toward a new mode of being in which the self relates itself to its own self. Freud's naturalistic perspective caused him to continually interpret the power of being in naturalistic categories—the ego-instinct and the sex-instinct, the ego-libido and the object-libido—though he increasingly sought to take into account the historical dimension of human existence. Kierkegaard construed the power of being in historistic terms, but he was not oblivious to the natural origin of selfhood. Even the significance of the sexual is acknowledged in his concept of Spirit. Indeed, Spirit is first posited in the sexual. The presence of Spirit, or self-consciousness, in sexuality is manifested in bashfulness or shame. It is a "prodigious contradiction that the immortal spirit is characterized as sex" (*CoD*, 62), but this is its original form of expression. Actually, Spirit is present in sexuality as a task, a task which begins immediately. This task is not to deny the sexual but "to win it into conformity with the destiny of the spirit." Kierkegaard continues,

> The realization of this task is the triumph of love in a man in whom the spirit has triumphed in such a way that the sexual is forgotten and only remembered in forgetfulness. When this has come about, then sensuousness is transfigured into spirit. [*CoD,* 72]

Keeping in mind that he explicitly rejects the ascetic denial of the sexual, it is apparent that this transfiguration of the sexual into Spirit is the counterpart of Freud's sublimation of Libido into Eros. Thus, even for Kierkegaard the earliest manifestation of Spirit is the sexual; and conversely, the ultimate significance of the sexual is Spirit.

In conclusion, then, I wish to maintain that Libido is Spirit viewed from the perspective of nature, and Spirit is Libido viewed from the perspective of history. Freud's concept of Eros seeks to take into account this historical dimension of selfhood, but in the end it fails. Though it is a highly sublimated form of Libido, it fails to reach the sublime heights of Agape, which is Kierkegaard's understanding of love.[1] In Eros the self remains in bondage to itself, for the locus of its concern is its own selfhood. In Agape the self is freed from this bondage when the locus of its concern shifts to the selfhood of others. Thus the self which exists in Agape reaches the most sublime form of selfhood; through the paradox of losing its self, it finds its self.[2]

The Structure of Selfhood

The dialectic of selfhood may be variously described. It may be analyzed with respect to its essential structure or its exis-

1. See Kierkegaard's *Works of Love* (New York: Harper & Row, 1962).

2. See Marcuse, *Eros and Civilization,* p. 114. Marcuse suggests that the subordination of Eros to Logos transforms Eros into Agape.

tential actualization or its ultimate norm. When Kierkegaard
sets forth the essential structure of the self, he does so in terms
of the "immediate self," the "mediate self," and the "theological self." Freud, on the other hand, develops a "topography"
of the mind in which selfhood is understood as a dynamic
relationship between the id, the ego, and the superego. An
investigation of the relationship between these two conceptions of the structure of selfhood follows.

For Kierkegaard the self is essentially dialectical in character.
The self, as he never tires of reminding us, is a relation which
relates itself to its own self. More explicitly, "The self is the
conscious synthesis of infinitude and finitude which relates
itself to itself, whose task is to become itself, a task which can
be performed only by means of a relationship to God" (*SuD*,
162). When Kierkegaard speaks of the self as a synthesis of the
infinite and the finite, he means that the self is a continual
dialectic between the expansive, "infinitizing" impulse, and
the limiting, "finitizing" tendency. The infinitizing factor is
Spirit which continually projects before the self its infinite
possibilities. But, unless this impulse is related to the finite
possibilities which immediately confront it, the self can be lost
in fantasy. Kierkegaard illustrates this with respect to feeling,
knowing, and willing. Selfhood can be lost in sentimental emo-
tion, irrelevant knowledge, and impractical intention. Without
the infinitizing power of Spirit, however, selfhood would just
as certainly be lost in unimaginative immediacy. Thus, selfhood is a dialectic of the Spirit. The self is a relation which
consciously relates the infinitizing Spirit to finite, realistic
ends.

Freud considers the self to be essentially dualistic in character. His earliest formulation of the dualistic interpretation of
the self was that of a relationship between the primary ψ-
system and the secondary ψ-system. Libido is the fundamental
power of the primary ψ-system. Indeed, it is the essential
psychic reality. It arises from the basic biological and psychological needs of the organism, but, unless a second mental

activity is superimposed upon this wishful activity, the self will be lost in hallucination. The secondary ψ-system has the function of inhibiting or limiting the infinite desires of the primary ψ-system and of relating them to realistic objects of gratification. In Kierkegaard's terms, the self is seen to be a relationship between the infinitizing instinctual desires of the primary ψ-system and the finitizing inhibitions of the secondary ψ-system.

As we have seen, Freud's concept underwent continual evolution, but the dualistic principle of interpretation remained. In his early formulation the sex-instinct was the infinitizing factor and the ego-instinct the finitizing factor. Later this conceptualization was supplanted by another in which object-libido was the infinitizing element and ego-libido the finitizing. Finally, the essential dualism of the self was conceived in terms of Eros and Thanatos—Eros the infinitizing factor and Thanatos the finitizing factor. In this evolution we see Freud's struggle to be free from his naturalistic dualism, a movement in the direction of the dialectical conceptuality which is more amenable to the historical understanding of the self which Freud increasingly adopted.[3]

Freud's structural concepts underwent a similar evolution. The notion of a primary system of psychic drives overlaid by a secondary inhibiting system was later given its classical formulation in terms of the id and the ego. The processes of the id are understood to be totally unconscious, but the processes of the ego are differentiated by the criterion of consciousness. The term *ego* was reserved for those inhibitory processes which are truly conscious, and the term *superego* was given to the unconscious inhibitory processes. Thus the essential structure of the self comprises the id, the ego, and the superego. Through these structures operate the infinitizing power of

3. Norman O. Brown, in *Life Against Death* (Middletown, Conn.: Wesleyan University Press, 1959), pp. 77-86, also criticizes Freud's dualism and suggests that a dialectical ontology would have served him better.

being, Libido or Eros, and the finitizing power of nonbeing, Thanatos. The id is the locus of the infinitizing impulse; the ego, the locus of the finitizing impulse. Without the latter, selfhood would be dissipated in hallucinatory activity, or fantasy, as Kierkegaard expresses it. But without the former the self would return to the quiescent state of nonbeing.

The structure of the self is not as carefully delineated by Kierkegaard, but there is a striking similarity between the structures implicit in his analysis of selfhood and those explicitly developed by Freud. Kierkegaard posits a primal entity which he calls the "immediate self." With Freud, he notes that this is not yet a self, but an "it" or a "me," a "self in the dative case." This structure is itself composed of two elements, the body and the soul. But the relationship which exists between these elements is not sufficiently reflective to be called a "self." It is an immediate relation, a psychosomatic unity. This immediate self is identical with Freud's id. Operative within the immediate self is a third element, Spirit, which initially manifests itself as sexuality and ultimately calls into being a secondary structure which Kierkegaard calls the "mediate self" or the self, properly so-called. Again, the parallel with Freud is apparent. Eros, the fundamental power of being, is present in the id as Libido or the sex-instinct. But it ultimately necessitates the development of a secondary structure for which Freud reserves the designation *ego.* Finally, Kierkegaard points to a third structure, a "transcendent self" which constitutes the infinite or ideal self. This structure he calls the "theological self," without which the self could not become a self. The theological self functions as a God-concept by means of which the mediate self relates itself to its own self. It functions as a norm or telos, a referent for the mediate self. Freud's superego is surely a correlate. Indeed, in his critique of religion, this is precisely the locus of the religious phenomena, and the God-concept is treated as a kind of cosmic superego. Like Kierkegaard's theological self, Freud's superego exercises a certain censorship or judgment which carries the force of a "divine imperative."

Again, the complementary relationship of the two perspectives is apparent. Freud provides a thorough grounding in nature for Kierkegaard's highly historistic treatment of the self. And Kierkegaard provides a needed corrective to Freud's naturalistic tendency to strip the self of the very thing which gives the self its selfhood: freedom or self-determination. Kierkegaard acknowledges the fundamental psychosomatic origin of the self, but he does nothing to explicate the fact. Freud's treatment of the id processes supplies the lack. On the other hand, Freud acknowledges the historical dimension of selfhood in his concept of the ego and the superego, but his naturalistic reduction of the processes of the ego threatens to subvert the insight. Kierkegaard makes a significant contribution to the ego psychology neglected by Freud.

The Dynamics of Selfhood

The self or ego is essentially a dialectical relation between the infinitizing impulse of the Spirit or Eros and the finitizing inertia of Spiritlessness or Thanatos. Or, expressed in terms of the structures of selfhood, the self or ego is a dialectical relationship between the immediate self or id and the transcendent self or superego. This is the essence of selfhood. The problem of its existence must now be considered in the problem of becoming the self it essentially is. How does the self become a self, by necessity or in freedom? What are the dynamics involved in that becoming? With respect to Kierkegaard, it is apparent that the self comes into being in freedom, for freedom is the very essence of selfhood. But Freud is apparently a thoroughgoing determinist. He has done more than anyone else to document empirically the deterministic understanding of the self. Can these two positions be reconciled?

Kierkegaard is most helpful here in defining our terms and delineating their appropriate applicability. *Becoming,* he notes, is a change in existence, not in essence. The essence of the self is necessary by definition; its existence is not. It may well be that the essence of selfhood is a relation which relates itself to its own self; this may be true by definition—a tautology. But while this dialectical relationship is necessary if the self is to be a self, its existence is not a necessity but a possibility. Becoming, therefore, has to do not with essence but existence. It has to do with the transition from possibility to actuality, and this transpires in freedom. Otherwise, it is not a becoming at all.

Kierkegaard goes on to distinguish two kinds of becoming: a "first becoming" or natural becoming, and a "second becoming" or historical becoming. The first becoming lends itself to a deterministic interpretation, for it is a becoming which has already become. It is a becoming whose history is all past. But even so, the fact that it has become points to its coming into existence historically, i.e. in freedom. The second becoming is historical in the stricter sense of the word. "The more specifically historical becoming comes into being by the operation of a relatively free cause, which in turn points ultimately to an absolutely free cause" (*PF,* 62-63).

In applying this to becoming a self, it may be said that the essence of selfhood is necessary—by definition—but its existence is simply a possibility. The transition from possibility to actuality transpires with a relative freedom which points to an absolutely free cause. In the process of becoming a self, the self passes through two stages: a first becoming in which the immediate self comes into being, and a second becoming in which the mediate self comes into being. The immediate self comes into being "by nature," as we say, by which we mean by necessity. Actually, as Kierkegaard has shown, even this immediate self has come into being in freedom; but its actuality gives the illusion of necessity. The mediate self, on the other hand, comes into being historically, i.e. in freedom.

The translation of the dynamics of becoming into Freudian

categories is apparent. In Freud's theoretical system, the ego as well as the id comes into being by necessity. Where the id is determined by nature, the ego is determined by history. In either case we have a deterministic interpretation of selfhood: naturalistic determinism in the case of the id, historical determinism in the case of the ego. But this very distinction indicates Freud's recognition of the two becomings. The becoming of the id is a natural becoming; the becoming of the ego, an historical one. His naturalistic perspective, however, fails to do justice to the latter. His error in the latter case is an extension of his error in the former. As Kierkegaard points out, the first becoming gives the illusion of necessity because its becoming has already become. Its future has become past, possibility has become necessity, history has become nature. All that remains is retrospect. In retrospect we can discern the specific causes which contributed to the actualization of this particular entity and so, with a pseudowisdom born of hindsight, we can declare that the id has come into being by necessity. But in prospect it was not necessary that the psychosomatic entity we call the id come into being at all. This is also Freud's error with regard to becoming a self or an ego. In retrospect, the specific factors which contributed to the character of this present self appear as determinants; in prospect, they were alternatives. Which is to say: retrospectively the self is determined; prospectively it is free. Freud took the retrospective view; Kierkegaard, the prospective.

And which is right? Again, I would maintain a binoptic perspective. In the existential moment of decision, Kierkegaard is right: the self becomes a self in freedom. But by the same token Freud is right: that existential choice becomes one's past, which does indeed determine the alternatives available in the next existential moment. If possibility is ignored, selfhood ossifies in necessity, for a self which is wholly determined is no self at all. If necessity is ignored, selfhood is vaporized in possibility, for a self which is indeterminant can never become a definite self. Kierkegaard knew this, of course, and expressed it in the existential dialectical relation between necessity and possibility. Freud documented the necessary and Kierkegaard underscored the possible. But selfhood consists in a dialectical relation between the two, between the self one has become and the self he may yet be.

Having dealt with the logic of the transition from essential selfhood to existential selfhood, let us turn to the dynamics of the process. The essence of selfhood, as we have seen, is a dialectical relation between the finite and the infinite. The transition whereby this·essential self becomes actual, however, is accomplished by sustaining a dialectical relation between necessity and possibility. In structural terms, this is a dialectic between the immediate self and the transcendent self, or in Freud's terminology, between the id and the superego. What is the process whereby the transcendent pole, without which there could be no existential dialectic, comes to be?

For Kierkegaard, imagination is the medium through which Spirit exercises its infinitizing function and projects before the self its infinite possibilities. By means of the imagination an image of the possible or ideal self is set before the self. This self is not the self. It is the imaged possibility of the self, a transcendent ideal which makes it possible for the self to assume a relation to itself and so become a self. Without this ideal image of a possible self, the reflexive relationship which is the essence of selfhood would never come to be, and selfhood would be lost in immediacy. Imagination, then, supplies the possibility which enables the necessary to become actual.

Freud contributes greatly to our understanding of the existential dialectic in his concept *identification.* The content of the imaged self, of which Kierkegaard speaks, is acquired through the child's identification with his parents. Their values supply the substance of his ideal-ego. His image of his parents becomes the ideal image of the self by means of which he finds his identity. Introjected as a structure of the self, it becomes the superego or *Überich,* the "I" which is above the "I." This is an important step in the transition from essence to existence, for the institution of the superego makes it possible for the ego to assume a relation to its own self, to determine which impulses it will indulge and what means of fulfillment it will permit. The superego provides a referent for the ego's existential decisions.

The complementary relationship of Kierkegaard and Freud is apparent. Both are aware of the reflexive character of selfhood and understand that this relation of the self to itself is possible only by means of a transcendent image of the self. But Kierkegaard's intuitive insight into the process of imagination is greatly augmented by Freud's empirical investigation of the phenomenon of identification. Once again the difference is perspectival, disclosing different aspects of the same phenomenon. Freud's determinism is stretched from the naturalistic to the historical; however, his ontological presuppositions will not permit him to appropriate fully the spiritual dimension of the self. On the other hand, Kierkegaard's ontological commitment to Spirit, or freedom, prohibits an adequate appreciation of the deterministic factors in the dialectic of selfhood. But, as Kierkegaard's own intuition told him, genuine selfhood is a dialectic between the two.

The Reality of Selfhood

For Kierkegaard, the ultimate reality to which the self relates itself, and in relation to which it finds its own reality, is God. Freud was a militant atheist. To the multifarious attacks on the existence of God he added another. Where Kant cast into doubt the rational arguments for God but reinstated Him on the basis of a moral argument, Freud undermined even this basis for belief. He pointed out the immanental source of the categorical imperative and left man with an illusory god which is but the projection of his own wishes. Once again, can two such disparate positions be reconciled?

Both Kierkegaard and Freud understand the reality of the self to be contingent upon the reality to which the self relates itself. Thus, for both, there is an ontological gradient in self-hood corresponding to the ontological status of the reality to which the self is related. We have referred to this earlier as a successively modified structure which begins with the immediate self (the id), becomes the mediate self (the ego), and culminates in the transcendent self (the superego). The fundamental structure of selfhood remains the same: the self is a relation which relates itself to itself, a relation which is accomplished only by means of a relation to a reality which transcends the self. The nature of this reality and the consequent modes of selfhood contingent upon our understanding of it must now be examined. Once again we will note a striking parallel between Kierkegaard and Freud.

Both delineate a primal mode of being in which there is no transcendental referent. For Kierkegaard this is the "immediate self"; for Freud the "id." Both acknowledge that in fact such a self is not really a self, but an "it." In this mode of being there is no self and no self-consciousness; the reflexive relation which is the essence of selfhood has not yet emerged. This is because there is as yet no consciousness of any reality outside the self. It is completely determined by immanental forces, or what Freud terms "psychic reality." In Kierkegaard's words, such a man is "soulishly determined in immediate unity with his natural condition" (*CoD,* 37). Or again, "the sensuous and the psycho-sensuous completely dominate him" (*SuD,* 176). The id, as Freud would call it, is wholly determined by its psychosomatic needs. Both Kierkegaard and Freud acknowledge that this mode of being is really just a theoretical construct which has no existential exemplification. It is a logically implicit, but existentially transient, moment. The best example is the infant who responds immediately to its organic condition by kicking and crying with as yet not even the awareness of what it needs. Unless such a being relates itself to a reality outside itself, it will perish.

True selfhood emerges only with self-consciousness, only when the self consciously relates itself with its immediate needs to a reality outside itself. When this reality is perceived as "material reality," as Freud terms it, the most primitive mode of selfhood emerges. Kierkegaard calls it "aesthetic existence," for its ultimate referent is its own *pathos*. The fundamental principle by which it exists is the pleasure principle, modified by the reality principle, where reality is construed as material objects of gratification. Such a self exists in the categories of pleasure/unpleasure, *(Lust/Unlust)* as Freud puts it. Or in Kierkegaard's words, "Its dialectic is: the agreeable and the disagreeable; its concepts are: good fortune, misfortune, fate" *(SuD,* 184). This mode of existence is fundamental to all others; the self could not exist at all without a relation to its material world. However, its ontological status is limited by the reality to which it relates itself. Material reality does not exhaust the ontological context in which the self exists.

In addition to material reality there is also a social reality. Not only does the self exist in a world of nature, it also exists in an historical world. The self is not fully a self apart from its relation to this realm of its reality, as well as to the realm of nature. Freud takes this into account in his concept of the superego in which the social ideal is incorporated into the structures of the self. This historical self, then, is the self which relates the id to the superego. Kierkegaard calls this mode "ethical existence," for its ultimate referent is the *ethos* of its culture. Such a self exists in the categories guilty/not-guilty. To be sure, this mode of existence has a higher ontological status than the aesthetic; it takes into account a far more comprehensive reality, and the degree of self-consciousness is intensified. But for Kierkegaard this is still a self whose measure is man, a self whose possibility is still a finite determinate ideal, and hence a self which is not yet fully a self. Such a self has found a degree of freedom from naturalistic determinism, only to find itself caught in the relativities of historical determinism.

As we have seen, Kierkegaard was aware of the natural self and the historical self, but he was also aware of what he calls

the "theological self" (*SuD,* 210). He could accept Freud's ego
as the structure by means of which the self relates itself to its
natural world; he could also accept the superego as the structure by means of which the self relates itself to its historical
world; but he would also insist upon the theological self as the
structure whereby the self relates itself to a transcendent reality. While it is true, as Freud points out, that the self cannot
survive unless its somatic desires are related to a realistic object
of gratification, it is also true, as Kierkegaard makes clear, that
the self whose desire is exhausted in material things has lost its
selfhood in natural determinism. While it is true, as Freud says,
that the self must relate itself to its social environment, it is
also true, as Kierkegaard insists, that selfhood is lost in cultural
determinism if the prevailing mores become absolutely normative. It is only when the self relates itself to a genuinely transcendent reality that the dialectic of selfhood is kept open and
the self continues to become a self. Kierkegaard calls this
mode of existence "religious existence," for its ultimate referent is *theos,* God. Such a self exists in the categories faith/un-
faith.

Freud was aware of the ultimate inadequacy of social reality.
This is clear from his discussion of the neurotic culture. We
can make adequate judgments concerning the selfhood of an
individual vis-à-vis the social norm, but what if the society
itself is neurotic? And how would we know if it was? In this
dilemma, Freud's response was a counsel of despair. For one
whose self-confessed god is Ananke (necessity), there is no
way out of the dilemma. To be sure, he offers a dialectical
resolution: reason within the limits of necessity. But on such
grounds there is ultimately no such thing as selfhood. There is
only a psychosomatic organism responding to the dual determinism of nature and history—and even history is reduced to
nature.

Kierkegaard's words concerning necessity have a peculiar
relevance to Freud. "The fatalist is in despair—he has lost God,
and therefore himself as well; for if he has not God, neither

has he a self. But the fatalist has no God—or, what is the same thing, his god is necessity" (*SuD*, 173). Kierkegaard offers an alternative solution. In place of necessity, he offers possibility as the ultimate reality. God is *possibility*, and selfhood consists in a continual relationship to the possible. In relation to possibility, or freedom, the relativity of every cultural norm is disclosed. This does not mean that Kierkegaard utterly rejects the value of the cultural ideal. Indeed, without it the self would be lost in the abyss of the infinite, the possible, and the eternal. The problem of relating to that which is Wholly Other is given a dialectical resolution.

Spirit projects its reality in the form of an ideal image of the self, an image that bears its culture's content. It is not God, for the ultimate power of being is Spirit, but it is an image of God. And, as the imaged possibility of the self, it exercises a God-function in the dialectic of selfhood. It is not surprising, then, that God would be given an anthropomorphic image. But, as Freud was quick to see, it is patently infantile to confuse the image with the reality. With Kierkegaard, he saw that freedom is ultimately possible only by means of a relation to a transcendent ideal, but he despaired of such an ideal. He saw that a relation to a finite God is just an illusory freedom, but he did not see that the finite can become an image of the infinite.

Here Kierkegaard's dialectical insight is needed. Selfhood is lost in an abyss of infinitude and possibility without a relation to a specific God; yet, selfhood is equally lost when its specific image of God becomes opaque to the Wholly Other. When reality is seen to be infinite, eternal possibility, the dialectic of selfhood is never closed, and the self continues to become a self.

Part Two
The Loss of
Selfhood

4. Kierkegaard's Concept of Despair

The Sickness unto Death

The first section of this treatise dealt with the notion of "being," not being itself, but one peculiar form of being— *human* being. In this section I will consider the problem of nonbeing, again in one specific form—*human* nonbeing. Since the mode of being peculiar to man is selfhood, this section will be concerned with nonbeing as the loss of selfhood.

As we have seen, Kierkegaard construed selfhood to be a function of Spirit, a kind of ego-instinct, an impulse inherent in the human being toward freedom or self-determination. Spirit is a self-reflexive impulse, an impulse of the self to relate itself to its self or to assume responsibility for itself. It is present in the human being from birth as an unrealized potentiality, a task to be performed, a possibility to be actualized. But the realization of this mode of being does not transpire with necessity. Selfhood comes into being in freedom or it does not come into being at all, for an unfree self is a contradiction in terms. The process whereby the self becomes a self is the dialectic of Spirit. The self becomes a self by relating itself to a reality beyond itself. The degree of selfhood which the self realizes is dependent upon the norm or referent to which the self relates itself. We have seen the gradient of realities which the self may choose as its ultimate referent, and the degrees of being or selfhood which result from such a choice. The choice of material reality as one's frame of reference produces aesthetic existence. The choice of social reality results in ethical existence. The choice of Spirit itself as the ultimate reality results in the authentic mode of selfhood which Kierkegaard calls religious existence. Such a mode of being is never static; it is an endless dialectic. As such, selfhood requires the self to continually sustain a dialectical relation between the finite and the infinite, necessity and possibility, the temporal and the eternal.

Inasmuch as the self, or human being, is essentially a relation, nonbeing is a disrelationship in the relation. Kierkegaard calls this disrelationship *despair*. "Despair is the disrelationship in a relation which relates itself to itself" (*SuD,* 148). Despair, he adds, is a "sickness unto death." Since life, or being, is a synthesis of the immediate self with a transcendent reality, death, or nonbeing, is the vitiation of this synthesis.

What is it that makes despair a continual possibility? Despair is not inherent in human nature. If it were, "it would not be despair, it would be something that befell a man, something he suffered passively . . . like death which is the lot of all"(*SuD,* 148-49). But while despair is not inherent in human existence, the possibility of despair is. "Whence then comes despair?" Kierkegaard asks. "From the relation wherein the synthesis relates itself to itself, . . . that is, in the fact that the relation relates itself to itself" (*SuD,* 149). It is therefore from this fact—that man is the kind of being who is himself responsible for his own being—that despair is an ever-present possibility.

Although despair is not a necessary condition of human existence, it is universal. Kierkegaard contends, "There lives not one single man who after all is not to some extent in despair" (*SuD,* 155). This is understandable when we recall the various types of despair. First there is a despair which is "unconscious that it is despair" (*SuD,* 175). Such a despair has nothing to do with a psychological mood or feeling, of course. It is a mode of being. Here there is no selfhood nor even any consciousness of having a self. One is in despair precisely because there is no self-consciousness. However, there is a higher mode of despair:

despair which is conscious of being despair. This despair is more intensive, for it is conscious of being despair. But, by the same token, selfhood is present in this type of despair. Kierkegaard distinguishes two kinds of conscious despair: the "despair of weakness," and the "despair of defiance" (*SuD*, 182ff., 200ff.). The former is that condition in which the self is aware of Spirit but is too weak to break with immediacy and relate itself to a transcendent referent of any sort, and so it does not become a self. There is an ironic heightening of this despair when such an individual is in despair over his weakness. Finally, there is the despair of defiance in which the individual is aware of Spirit, and hence of its self, but dissociates itself from every transcendent referent. It constructs its own reality and defiantly seeks to become the self it wills to be. This is the highest degree of self-consciousness but, consequently, also the most intense despair, for the self is not a self and it is intensely conscious of that fact. In each of these cases, the self is not a self because there is a disrelation in the relationship which constitutes selfhood.

It is important to investigate the conditions under which the fall from potential being to actual nonbeing takes place. But how shall we conduct such an investigation? What approach is valid for understanding despair? The difficulty, Kierkegaard points out, is that each approach brings with it its own "mood," and this mood, if inappropriate to the subject under consideration, can alter the concept. The proper mood in which to comprehend despair is existential seriousness (*CoD*, 13). Any other approach distorts our understanding of it.

To attempt to comprehend the transition from being to nonbeing aesthetically is to distort the mood into either the comic or the tragic. If we speculate that the transition takes place by deliberate rational choice, the mood is changed from the serious to the comic, for no one could seriously choose the agony of despair. On the other hand, if we speculate that the transition takes place by necessity, the mood is changed to the tragic. Aesthetics founders on the reality of guilt.

Kierkegaard claims that ethics comes closer to being the proper science for the study of despair, for it takes seriously the reality of guilt. But ethics, too, is the wrong approach. Intent upon actualizing the ideal and thereby remaining innocent, ethics founders on the reality of sin. Ethics forgets that sin is not merely the occasional violation of the ethical norm but the very presupposition of that violation. The ethical explanation of the transition from being to nonbeing presupposes the fall; it does not explain it. "Sin withdraws deeper and deeper as a deeper and deeper presupposition, as a presupposition which goes well beyond the individual" (CoD, 17).

Even when psychology attempts to deal with despair, the concept becomes distorted, for the mood of psychology is objective. Despair is not a psychological state; it is a mode of being. Ultimately the concept of despair is not the proper subject for any science; no science can explain the transition from being to nonbeing. But psychology can do the next best thing. It can study the psychological state which is the presupposition of despair—the state Kierkegaard calls "dread." Yet he warns us against assuming that it *explains* the fall. "Psychology can only explain up to the explanation" (CoD, 35).

The Concept of the Fall

Dread: The Presupposition of the Fall

Kierkegaard's analysis of the problem of despair or sin takes the form of a psychological interpretation of the Adamic myth. His is a radical reinterpretation, however. He rejects any explanation which makes Adam a hypothetical person and thus unlike the rest of the human race. To explain the origin of sin by creating an individual who begins his existence in an entirely different condition than do subsequent men is not to explain sin at all. In such an explanation, sin is sin only for Adam; in all subsequent men sin is a given condition of their existence for which they bear no responsibility. Any explanation, to be an explanation, must explain the origin of sin in each individual and not by positing a different kind of person who first fell. Adam was ontologically no different from any other man; he was simply the first by accident. To posit Adam as different in kind is to postpone the problem of sin to the second man who is really human (*CoD*, 31). Thus Kierkegaard interprets the Adamic myth as the story of every man.

In Kierkegaard's interpretation the primal state is innocence and the transition from innocence to guilt does not transpire by necessity. When one speaks of innocence as though it were a phase in a natural process—a mode of being which passes in the natural course of events—he is no longer speaking about innocence. The concept of necessity belongs to logic; innocence is an ethical category. And, "it is unethical to say that innocence must be annulled *(aufgehoben)*, for it can only be annulled by guilt." (*CoD*, 32).

In the Adamic myth innocence is ignorance. The primal state is characterized by the ignorance of good and evil. "In his innocence man is not determined as spirit but is soulishly determined in immediate unity with his natural condition" (*CoD*, 37). That is to say, there is as yet no knowledge of good and evil; man's behavior is determined by his natural impulses. Still primal man is not merely an animal, for Spirit is latently present in him. Kierkegaard notes:

> In the state of innocence man is not merely an animal, for if at any time of his life he was merely an animal, he never would become a man. So then the spirit is present, but in a state of immediacy, a dreaming state. [*CoD*, 39]

Man's innocence, he adds, is "not an animal brutality but an ignorance which is qualified by spirit" (*CoD*, 40).

In a sense this ignorance is also despair. It is "despair which is unconscious that it is despair," or "the despairing unconsciousness of having a self" (*SuD*, 175). Kierkegaard notes, "The minimum of despair is a state which . . . by reason of a sort of innocence does not even know that there is such a

thing as despair" (*SuD*, 175). And yet he confesses that this is
"despair improperly so called" (*SuD*, 146). Improper because
in the state of innocence Spirit is yet dreaming. Despair can
only occur in freedom, so, until Spirit is awakened, despair is
an inappropriate designation.

Continuing with his interpretation of the Adamic myth,
Kierkegaard seeks to understand how potential Spirit becomes
actual, ignorance becomes knowledge, and innocence becomes
guilt. As we have already seen, he rejects the aesthetic way of
handling the transition. "In a logical system it is convenient
enough to say that possibility passes over into actuality. In
reality it is not so easy, and an intermediate determinant is
necessary. This intermediate determinant is dread" (*CoD*, 44).
Following the Genesis account, Kierkegaard notes that to this
state of innocence there comes an enigmatic word, the word of
prohibition. "The prohibition alarms Adam [induces a state of
dread] because the prohibition awakens in him the possibility
of freedom . . . the alarming possibility of *being able"* (*CoD*,
40). What he is able to do is not specified. It is an unspecified
ability, "a nothing vaguely hinted at" (*CoD*, 38). It is simply
the possibility of being able, the possibility of freedom. The
prohibition awakens the individual to a consciousness of a
possible mode of being where it (the individual) is no longer
determined by nature, but is responsible for its own existence.

The possibility of existence in freedom evokes an ambiguous
response. There is a fascination with this possibility, and yet
there is also a dread. One is attracted to this mode of being,
yet at the same time one is terrified by it. The biblical account
expresses the threatening character of freedom in the word of
judgment which follows the word of prohibition: "Thou shalt
surely die." That is to say, with the realization of the possibility of freedom there comes a realization of the possibility of
despair, the sickness unto death. In the primal state, there was
no threat of death, for there was no awareness of life. Now
there are both. Just as the prohibition awakens in man the
awareness of a new mode of being which fascinates and in-

trigues him, so the word of judgment awakens a "deterring conception" (*CoD*, 41). The prohibition awakens the fascinating dread of being able which is immediately followed by the repelling dread of death. The dread which the possibility of freedom evokes is therefore an ambiguous dread. As Kierkegaard expresses it, "Dread is a *sympathetic antipathy and an antipathetic sympathy"* (*CoD*, 38).

Guilt: The Consequence of the Fall

Now the transition from innocence to guilt is clear, but only "up to the explanation." To man in the state of innocence there comes a prohibiting word which awakens him to the possibility of existence in freedom. He is fascinated by the possibility, yet terrified. He is filled with an ambiguous dread. But dread is not guilt. Dread is not wrong, for it is the inevitable concomitant of freedom. Still one becomes guilty in the moment of dread. In this moment innocence is lost. How this happens "psychology is unable to explain, for it is the qualitative leap" (*CoD*, 43). Nevertheless, Kierkegaard gives us a kind of dramatic unpacking of that moment:

> One may liken dread to dizziness. He whose eye chances to look down into the yawning abyss becomes dizzy. But the reason for it is just as much his eye as it is the precipice. For suppose he had not looked down. Thus dread is the dizziness of freedom which occurs when the spirit would posit the synthesis, and freedom then gazes down into its own possibility, grasping at finiteness to sustain itself. In this dizziness freedom succumbs. Further than this psychology cannot go and will not. That very instant everything is changed, and when freedom rises again it sees that it is guilty. Between these two instants lies the leap, which no science has explained or can explain. He who becomes guilty in dread becomes as ambiguously guilty as it is possible to be. Dread is a womanish debility in which freedom swoons. Psychologically speaking, the fall into sin always

occurs in impotence. But dread is at the same time the most egoistic thing, and no concrete expression of freedom is so egoistic as is the possibility of every concretion. This again is the overwhelming experience which determines the individual's ambiguous relation, both sympathetic and antipathetic. In dread there is the egoistic infinity of possibility, which does not tempt like a definite choice, but alarms and fascinates with its sweet anxiety. [*CoD*, 55]

Kierkegaard is saying here that the prohibition awakens man to the possibility of freedom, but the awareness of this possibility creates the dizziness of dread and man grasps about him for something to make him feel secure, something to relieve him of the awful responsibility of freedom. In that instant he becomes guilty, for in that instant he became responsible. He could no longer innocently obey his instincts with a kind of irresponsibility. He was free, but he could not endure that freedom. He sought an escape from freedom, but he cannot escape the guilt.

The guilt which he experiences is not ultimately explainable. "Psychologically speaking, the fall into sin always occurs in impotence," and yet man is guilty. "He who becomes guilty in dread becomes as ambiguously guilty as it is possible to be," for, as Kierkegaard says elsewhere, "He who through dread becomes guilty is innocent, for it was not he himself but dread, an alien power which laid hold of him, a power which he loved and yet dreaded—and yet he is guilty, he who after all loved it while he feared it" (*CoD*, 39). He is guilty because when Spirit projected its own reality—freedom, as the proper mode of human existence—he chose to give up that freedom and thereby his self.

This *choice* is not the rational deliberation that is usually meant by the term, an objective decision between two alternatives. This choice "does not tempt like a definite choice, but alarms and fascinates with its sweet anxiety" (*CoD*, 55). Nevertheless it is a choice. There are alternatives: being and nonbeing. And the individual participates in the decision with his whole being. It is an active, not a passive, experience for which the individual is himself responsible. To suggest that he becomes guilty passively does not account for the overwhelming sense of personal responsibility which accompanies the experience of guilt. It is therefore an existential choice in which the individual is responsible for the loss of his essential freedom. The choice in which he flees from freedom is itself an affirmation of freedom. Before the original choice in which Spirit is affirmed, there is no freedom. There is only the possibility of freedom. This possibility the individual experiences as dread. The action whereby he flees from this possibility is the choice in which he both affirms his freedom and rejects it.

The Object of Dread

Despair, or sin, is the flight response of the individual to the dread of freedom. But, strangely enough, flight does not seem to eliminate dread. If it is the possibility of freedom which provokes dread, the renunciation of freedom should mean the elimination of dread. In fact, however, dread persists. Kierkegaard notes, "Sin entered by dread, but sin in turn brought dread with it" (*CoD,* 70). Dread, then, is both the presupposition and the consequence of sin. How is this so?

In Adam, which is to say in the state of innocence, dread was a dread of the "nothing." It was a dread of a mere possibility, the possibility of freedom. But, with the fall into nonbeing, the nothing of dread becomes a "something." Dread becomes a dread of something; it becomes objective. In the fallen state men identify some particular condition with sinfulness; they name their nameless dread. Then dread persists, not in the vague uneasiness which is characteristic of dread, but in the specific anxiety of objective dread. Illustrations follow.[1]

Sinfulness is commonly identified with the sensuous. The sensuous or sexuality becomes the object of dread. Kierke-

1. The following discussion is derived from *The Concept of Dread,* pp. 70-72.

gaard suggests that this can be understood against the background of the essential dialectic. Essentially man is a dialectic of the finite and the infinite, a synthesis of the finite body and soul—sustained by the self in relation to Spirit. If Spirit is rejected, man is "soulishly determined"; the sensuous dominates his existence. Thus the sensuous comes to signify spiritlessness or sin. The most obvious manifestation of the sensuous is the sexual, so sexuality comes to be identified with sin and becomes the object of dread.

Similarly, egoism has come to be identified with sin. But, Kierkegaard warns, "If one does not first make clear to oneself what 'self' means, there is not much use in saying of sin that it is selfishness" (*CoD*, 70). He adds, "The definition of sin as egoism may be quite correct, [but] . . . at the same time . . . it is so empty of content that it means nothing at all" (*CoD*, 69). Again, this objectification of dread in terms of egoism can be understood when examined under the rubric of the existential dialectic. Essentially man is a self; but unless the self relates itself to a transcendent reality it cannot become a self. When the self as a relationship is vitiated by the flight of dread, the undialectical "self" is estranged from its true reality. This condition, this undialectical "selfhood," is the egoism which signifies the absence of Spirit and therefore comes to be identified with sin, and egoism becomes the object of dread.

Again, the temporal has come to be equated with sin. Kierkegaard says, as we have already seen, that the synthesis of the soulish and the bodily is posited by Spirit and that this synthesis is accomplished only in relation to the eternal. Thus the self is a relation between the temporal and the eternal. But again it is dread which incites the individual to vitiate the relationship of selfhood. Thus, since the self is a synthesis of the temporal and the eternal, the loss of Spirit is reflected in the domination of the temporal. Consequently, the temporal comes to be equated with sin and becomes the object of dread.

The instant sin is posited, the temporal is sin. We do not

> say that the temporal is sinfulness, any more than that the
> sensuous is sinfulness; but for the fact that sin is posited
> the temporal signifies sinfulness. Therefore that man sins
> who lives merely in the instant abstracted from the eternal.
> [*CoD*, 82-83]

Thus we see that, while sin is originally the flight from freedom in dread, it may come to be identified with sexuality,
egoism, and the temporal.

The Potentiation of Despair

Dread of the Evil

The dialectic of dread is a progressively fatal disease, a sickness
unto *death* as Kierkegaard terms it. Not that this sickness
progresses as a matter of course, like a physical illness over
which one has no responsibility. Kierkegaard is quite clear
about this. The sickness unto death progresses always and only
by means of the individual's qualitative leap. But there is
nonetheless a dialectical progression to the sickness. As we
have seen, in the state of innocence the dread of possibility or
freedom results in a flight from freedom into bondage. The
aesthetic response would be that fate is responsible. The transition from freedom to bondage is inevitable; one must accept
it. But, as we have also seen, aesthetics founders on the reality
of guilt, and with the appearance of guilt we have the emergence of the ethical.

In the ethical response to despair, the individual is aware
that he is responsible for the loss of selfhood. To the dread of
freedom there is added the dread of guilt. In this state of
despair there is a longing for the state of innocence and a
dread of guilt. The individual wishes to be back where he was
before sin became an actuality. He seeks to return to the situation of innocence through the attitude of remorse; but remorse is unable to accomplish this. Remorse is itself the continuation of sin. It is unable to restore the lost freedom, for it

is never remorseful enough to repent. It must always await the sin; it can never precede it. Kierkegaard's sensitive description of the futility of remorse follows.

> Remorse cannot annul sin, it can only sorrow over it. Sin goes forward in its consequence, remorse follows it step by step, but always an instant too late. It compels itself to look at the horror, but it is like mad King Lear. . . . It has lost the reins of government and has strength left only to repine. Here dread is at its highest pitch. Remorse has lost its senses, and dread is potentiated to remorse. The consequence of sin goes on, it drags the individual with it as a woman is dragged by the hangman with his hand in her hair, while she shrieks in desperation. Remorse is in advance, it discovers the consequence before it comes, . . . the consequence comes nearer, the individual trembles. . . . Sin conquers. Dread throws itself despairingly into the arms of remorse. Remorse ventures its utmost. It interprets the consequence of sin as penal suffering, and perdition as a consequence of sin. It is lost, its doom is pronounced, its condemnation is certain, and the aggravation of the sentence is that the individual shall throughout his life be dragged to the place of execution. In other words, remorse has become insane. [*CoD,* 102-03]

Ethics seeks to get the individual in the right position with regard to sin, i.e. to make the individual see that he is guilty. As soon as this is accomplished, the individual stands remorseful in sin. But this is the contradiction of ethics. Since ethics requires the perfection of ideality, it must be content with remorse. This is the nearest it can come to ideality. Remorse delays the action required by ethics. In ethical existence the individual can never get beyond remorse. The only help in such a circumstance is that remorse become its own object and renounce itself. "At last remorse must become its own object, being remorseful for the fact that its movement becomes a deficit of action" (*CoD,* 105). But this is a new mode of response. It is no longer the ethical response of remorse, but the religious response of repentance. The dialectical apex of remorse takes place "where in posing [*sic*] itself it will annul itself by a new remorse [repentance] and then collapse" (*CoD*, 105).

Now, so long as the individual lives in dread of the evil, he may be said to be "in the good." That is, though the individual is in sin, the very fact that he dreads the evil is evidence that essentially the reality to which he relates himself is, as yet, the good. However, despair is a progressively fatal disease, a sickness unto death. First there is sin or despair, the flight from the good, from freedom. But despair is a pernicious thing; it can become a way of life. This despair is potentiated when the individual despairs over his condition, when he despairs of the possibility of freedom from despair. As Kierkegaard puts it:

> To indicate the character of this potentiation from sin to despair over sin one might say that the former is the breach with the good, the latter is the breach with repentance. Despair over sin is an attempt to maintain oneself by sinking still deeper. . . . Sin itself is the struggle of despair; but then when strength is exhausted there must needs be a new potentiation, a new demoniacal introversion, and this is despair over one's sin. . . . By despairing over his sin, and about the reality of repentance, about grace, he has also lost himself. [*SuD*, 240-41]

Kierkegaard speaks about the "continuity" of selfhood or the "consistency" of the self—that wherein the self consists, that which gives the self its continuity. Now the authentic mode of human being consists in existence qua Spirit. That is, true selfhood consists in continual self-consciousness, the continual relating of the self to itself and to something higher. Such a person is a saint, but even the sinner has his existence in the good so long as it is the evil which he dreads.

Every existence which is under the rubric of spirit . . . has essentially consistency within itself, and consistency in something higher, at least in an idea. But again such an existence fears infinitely every inconsistency, because it has an infinite conception of what the consequence may be, that because of it one might be wrenched out of the totality in which one has one's life. [*SuD*, 238]

The least inconsistency is a tremendous loss, for with it a man loses that in which his selfhood consists. The believer, for example, may also be a sinner, but because it is the good in which he has his consistency he lives in dread of every sin, for by every sin he loses his consistency, his self.

But, as it is with the believer, so it is with his counterpart, the demoniac. The demoniac has his consistency in the evil. He has given up the good. He has renounced existence qua Spirit and his consistency resides in spiritlessness. He lives, therefore, in dread of the good for it threatens the consistency of his existence. He experiences the good as a temptation, as that which threatens to destroy his mode of being, and so he lives in dread of freedom. Kierkegaard spells this out as follows:

Just because the demoniac is consistent in himself and in the consistency of evil, just for this cause he also has a totality to lose. A single instant outside of his consistency . . . and with that, he would never more be himself, he says. That is, he has given up the good in despair, it could not help him anyway, he says, but it well might disturb him, make it impossible for him ever again to acquire the full momentum of consistency, make him weak. Only in the continuation of sin he is himself. . . . What does this mean? It means that the state of being in sin is that which . . . holds him together. [*SuD*, 239]

Actually, both are compulsive modes of being; neither is free. When an individual has his consistency in the good, he lives in dread of the evil; he has an unfree relation to the evil. And, conversely, when an individual's consistency lies in the evil, he lives in dread of the good; he has an unfree relation to the good (*CoD*, 106). The former is the bondage of sin, the latter is the demoniacal. The former manifests itself in a compulsive moralism, the latter in a compulsive fatalism.

Dread of the Good

The demoniacal has been regarded from various standpoints. If it is approached from the aesthetic point of view, "the phenomenon then falls under the categories of misfortune, fate, etc., [it] can be regarded as analogous with congenital lunacy, etc." (*CoD*, 106). In such an approach, the relation of the observer to the phenomenon is one of "compassion." But compassion is of little help to the sufferer. It is rather a means of protecting one's own ego. One dare not identify too deeply with the sufferer, for fear of finding there himself. So he protects himself from this danger by distancing himself from it through compassion. In reality, this is a false compassion.

> Only when the compassionate person is so related by his compassion to the sufferer that in the strictest sense he comprehends that it is his own cause which is here in question, only when he knows how to identify himself in such a way with the sufferer that when he is fighting for an explanation he is fighting for himself, renouncing all thoughtlessness, softness, and cowardice, only then does compassion acquire significance. [*CoD*, 107]

The demoniacal has also been ethically regarded; from this viewpoint the observer is related to the phenomenon through "condemnation." Kierkegaard reminds us of the centuries in which the demoniac was treated with terrible severity for his "guilt." We may, in our enlightened age, look down on this mode of relating to the demoniac, but, Kierkegaard asks, is our "sentimental compassion so very much more commendable? ... The fact that it was so ethically severe shows precisely that its compassion was a better quality" (*CoD*, 108). The ethical person could find no other explanation for his identifying with the demoniac than guilt. And, in his compassion, he was convinced that every severity should be employed against the demoniac for his own sake.

Finally, the demoniacal has been regarded therapeutically. Here the relationship to the demoniac is "objectivity." The sufferer is regarded as an object, as it were. "The therapeutic way of viewing the case regards the phenomenon as purely physical and somatic," and seeks to remedy the problem *"mit Pulver und mit Pillen,"* as Kierkegaard satirically puts it. He concludes:

> The fact that such various ways of regarding it are possible shows how ambiguous is this phenomenon, and that in a way it belongs to all spheres, the somatic, the psychic, the pneumatic. . . . This can be explained by the fact that man is a synthesis of soul and body supported by spirit, wherefore a disorganization in one shows itself in the others. [*CoD,* 109]

Kierkegaard thus shows himself to be surprisingly contemporary in his holistic view of the demoniacal. He is not oblivious to the somatic and the psychic factors involved in the demoniacal, but he is convinced that the problem is essentially pneumatic. Essentially the demoniacal is the state of unfreedom. But freedom can be lost in different ways—somatic-psychically or pneumatically. The self is a relation of body and soul sustained by its relation to Spirit. Whenever the somatic element dominates the synthesis, the demonic is present. "So soon as the subordinate relation comes to an end, so soon as the body revolts, so soon as freedom enters into a conspiracy with it against itself, there unfreedom is present as the demoniacal" (*CoD,* 121). The demoniacal can manifest itself in a multitude of somatic-psychic ways: "an exaggerated sensibility, an exaggerated irritability, nervous affections, hysteria, hypochondria, etc." (*CoD,* 122). But the extreme form is what Kierkegaard calls "bestial perdition," which "shuns . . . every contact with the good, whether this actually threatens it by wanting to help it to freedom, or merely touches it quite casually" (*CoD*, 122).

Freedom may also be lost pneumatically. The demoniacal is a breakdown in the dialectic of Spirit. A diagnosis of the symptoms can be made in terms of the threefold dialectic of the self: the essential dialectic, the existential dialectic, and the ultimate dialectic. These correspond to the following symptoms: "the vacuous," "the shut-up," and "the sudden." I will begin with "shut-upness"—a manifestation of a breakdown in the existential dialectic of the self.

With respect to the elements of necessity and possibility, the demoniac has lost possibility or freedom. In freedom he has fled from freedom, and now his "selfhood" consists in sustaining that mode of being into which he has fled, namely, unfreedom or necessity. The demonic element in this mode of being is that it does not dread the state into which it has fallen, i.e. necessity, but dreads that which could set it free, i.e. possibility. "The demoniacal is dread of the good" (*CoD*, 109), that is, dread of freedom. This, we will recall, was also the situation in the state of innocence, but now with a difference. The state of innocence is "oriented towards freedom," whereas the demonic state is oriented toward unfreedom.

Still, freedom is present even in the unfreedom of the demoniacal. There is no dread except where there is freedom. So the response of dread, in the presence of the good, ironically reveals the presence of freedom. As Kierkegaard puts it, "Freedom lying prone in unfreedom revolts upon coming into communication with freedom outside and now betrays unfreedom in such a way that it is the individual who betrays himself against his will in dread" (*CoD*, 110). When freedom comes into contact with the demoniac, he becomes anxious and shuts himself up more and more within himself. But by so doing he unwittingly reveals his freedom.

With respect to the essential dialectic of the finite and the infinite, the demoniac has lost the infinite. He has lost his selfhood in the finite, "the vacuous," and he has lost his relationship to the infinite. What the shut-up dreads may not be known. What has instigated this "close reserve," this profound "introversion," may be a mystery. It may be "the most terrible thing or the most insignificant, the most appalling thing, the presence of which in life is perhaps not dreamt of by many, or the bagatelle to which nobody pays any attention" (*CoD,* 113), but, whatever it is, it is the finite that preoccupies the shut-up. With regard to the infinite, he is empty, "vacuous." That which now constitutes the meaning of his existence is meaninglessness.

Whatever would reveal the secret constitutes a terrible threat to the shut-up. It threatens to disclose the meaninglessness for what it is and, even though this would restore the possibility of a meaningful existence, it is experienced as a threat, for it places in jeopardy that in which the continuity of the "self" consists. The shut-up has many ways of dealing with this threat.

> Shut-upness may wish for revelation, wish that it might be effected from without, that this might happen to it. . . . It may will revelation to a certain degree, but keep back a little vestige, only to begin all over again with shut-upness. . . . It may will revelation, but *incognito* . . . Revelation may have already conquered, shut-upness ventures to employ its last expedient and is cunning enough to transform revelation itself into a mystification, and shut-upness has won. [*CoD,* 113-14]

How the individual responds to the revelation is crucial. That is, is he willing or unwilling to accept responsibility for that which is thus revealed? If he is unwilling, he remains in the demoniacal state.

> Even the man who merely wishes revelation is nevertheless essentially demoniacal. He has in fact two wills, one of them subordinate, impotent, which wills revelation, and a stronger will which wills to be shut up; but the fact that

this is the stronger shows that essentially he is demoniacal. [*CoD*, 115]

Again, as in the existential dialectic, the dread no less than the wish for revelation reveals the presence of the infinite which persists even in the bondage to the finite.

Finally, with respect to the ultimate dialectic of the temporal and the eternal, the demoniac has lost the eternal. He has lost his selfhood in the temporal. The shut-up has a kind of continuity like "the vertigo we may suppose a top must feel as it revolves perpetually upon its pivot" (*CoD*, 115), but unless he has become completely insane this egoistic continuity comes and goes. It is a temporal continuity. There is here no relation to the eternal and hence no eternal continuity. This "apparent continuity of close reserve will display itself as the sudden. One instant it is there, the next it is gone, and no sooner is it gone than it is there again" (*CoD*, 116). Kierkegaard suggests that the more the shut-up's freedom is expended in the process of maintaining the close reserve, the more certain it is that the secret will be revealed, however unwillingly. The most trivial incident may be sufficient to trigger the "terrible monologue" which speaks volumes about the shut-up's secret. Kierkegaard discerned the subtlety of this unfree revelation which can suddenly break out.

The ventriloquism may be plainly declarative, or it may be indirect, as when an insane man points to another person and says, "He is very objectionable to me, he's probably insane." Revelation may declare itself in words when the unfortunate man ends by intruding upon everyone his hidden secret. It may declare itself by a look, by a glance; for there is a glance of the eye by which a man involuntarily reveals what is hidden. There is an accusing glance which reveals what one almost dreads to understand; a contrite, imploring glance which hardly tempts curiosity to peer into this involuntary telegraphy. [*CoD*, 115]

Again, as with the other two dimensions of the dialectic of selfhood, the transcendent pole is present in its negated form. The eternal manifests itself in the sudden, the infinite manifests itself in the vacuous, and possibility manifests itself in shut-upness; but in each there remains the dread of the good.

Thus the progressive potentiation of despair reaches its utter depth. "First . . . sin was despair, its potentiation was despair over sin. But now God offers reconciliation in the forgiveness of sins. Yet the sinner despairs, and despair acquires a still deeper expression" (*SuD*, 245). The first is the dread of freedom, the next is dread of the evil, but the utmost despair is the despair of the good. In religious language, this is what Kierkegaard calls the sin against the Holy Spirit.

Cultural Manifestations of Despair

Every individual stands essentially in the place of Adam, with one difference: he exists in an historical nexus. Qualitatively the situation of every subsequent man is no different from Adam's; the transition from innocence to despair takes place by a "qualitative leap." That is, the individual himself posits the quality of his existence by his own decisive act. Quantitatively, however, there is a difference. The subsequent man exists in an historical nexus in which the nothing of dread has become more and more a something. While the quality of dread remains the same, i.e. the dread of freedom, quantitatively it is greater.

> Owing to the fact that the race does not begin afresh with every individual the sinfulness of the race acquires a history. This however proceeds by quantitative determinants, while the individual by the qualitative leap participates in it. The race therefore does not begin afresh with every individual, for in that way the race would be no race, but every individual begins afresh with the race. [*CoD*, 31-32]

In this manner Kierkegaard seeks to take cognizance of the collective character of despair without sacrificing the personal.

Not only does the cultural nexus contribute a quantitative increment to the dread which the individual experiences, but it also determines the form in which he encounters the dread of freedom and the manner in which he seeks to escape. Each culture posits its own reality, by means of which it seeks to escape from dread. But "the reality here posited is an illegitimate reality. So dread comes back again in relation to what was posited" (*CoD*, 99). Consequently, the form in which dread is encountered is determined by the individual's culture. Specifically, Kierkegaard cites the aesthetic culture in which dread is present in the form of fate, the ethical culture in which dread is present in the form of guilt, and the religious culture in which dread is present in the form of sin.

The Aesthetic Culture and the Concept of Fate

We have already seen that the essence of human existence is freedom or Spirit. But the concomitant of Spirit is dread. A culture which is without dread is spirit-less. Kierkegaard suggests that the most primitive culture may have approximated this condition. In such a culture human existence is defined as immediacy: man is determined by the immediately sensed desires. Here no dread exists for Spirit is not yet awakened. Nevertheless, dread lies hidden in the very possibility of freedom which such a primitive culture has not yet discovered.

> Even though in spirit-lessness there is no dread, because this is excluded just as spirit is, yet dread is there, nevertheless, only it is waiting. . . . Viewed from the standpoint of the spirit, dread is present in spirit-lessness, but hidden and masked. [*CoD*, 86]

Probably there exists no culture which is totally spirit-less. A modicum of self-consciousness is necessary for social existence. Herein lies the difference between spirit-lessness and paganism. As Kierkegaard puts it:

> In spirit-lessness there is no dread. It is too happy and content for that, and too spirit-less. But this is a pitiful reason, and in this respect paganism differs from spirit-lessness for the fact that it is oriented in the direction *towards* spirit, the other in the direction *away from it*. Paganism therefore, if you please, is absence of spirit, and as such it is very different from spirit-lessness. To that extent paganism is much to be preferred. Spirit-lessness is stagnation of the spirit.... Precisely in this consists its perdition, but also its sense of security, namely that it understands nothing spiritually, takes hold of nothing as a task. [*CoD,* 85]

In both the spirit-less culture and the pagan, Spirit is absent, but in the latter some awareness of Spirit is present even in its absence. Paganism, like spirit-lessness, "is sensuousness, but this is a sensuousness which has a relation to spirit, although the spirit in the deepest sense is not yet posited as spirit" (*CoD,* 86). In the spirit-less culture Spirit is present only as a potentiality, whereas in the pagan culture Spirit is present as fate. Not that fate is Spirit. Indeed, fate is the negation of Spirit. The pagan culture posits the reality of fate precisely in order to escape the demands of Spirit. Yet in that very act Spirit is present. In the spirit-less culture dread is present but waiting. But in the pagan culture dread has become objectified. Essentially dread has no object—it is simply the dread of freedom—but as soon as the possibility of freedom appears the pagan culture annuls it by supplanting Spirit with fate. Human existence is thus determined not in freedom but by fate. Whereas Spirit is the unity of necessity and possibility, fate is the unity of necessity and chance. Thus fate is the negation of Spirit; it is Spirit in which possibility has been reduced to chance. Even in the notion of fate, however, Spirit is present incognito. Its presence is disclosed by the presence of dread.

> In fate the dread of the pagan has its object. . . . The pagan
> cannot come into relation with fate, for one instant it is
> necessary, the next instant it is chance. And yet he is in
> relation to it, and this relation is dread. [*CoD,* 87]

The pagan's effort to establish a relationship with fate is seen
in his consultation with the oracle. To explain fate, the oracle
must be as ambiguous as fate. It must be able to mean one
thing and again to mean its opposite. And yet, the pagan is
bound by dread to the oracle; he dare not refrain from con-
sulting it. So his relation to fate is revealed as a relationship of
dread. Dread is present even in paganism, and Spirit is present,
although in the deepest sense Spirit is not yet posited as Spirit.
So dread is inescapable, for it returns in the form of that
which is posited as a means of escaping dread.

While the Greek culture is the paradigm of paganism for
Kierkegaard, paganism is not confined to ancient Greece.
Wherever Spirit is sacrificed to the security of fatalism paganism is present. Kierkegaard is quite aware of the existence of
paganism within Christendom. "Within Christianity," he says,
"the dread in relation to fate which is characteristic of paganism is found wherever spirit, though it is present, is not essentially posited as spirit" (*CoD,* 88). Christianity has been
known to forget its own insight and, like paganism, to posit
Spirit in the form of fate. But, in whatever guise paganism
appears, freedom is lost and with it selfhood.

The Ethical Culture and the Concept of Guilt

It is the reality of guilt which discloses the error of paganism.
Paganism simply cannot take guilt seriously. Indeed, the concept does not emerge in paganism, but "if it had emerged,
paganism would have foundered upon the contradiction that
one might become guilty by fate" (*CoD,* 87). If a person is
guilty, then according to the presuppositions of paganism he
has become so by fate. Yet to be guilty means precisely to be
individually responsible. This implies freedom, and freedom

annuls the concept of fate. In an aesthetic culture guilt is an impossibility for its categories are necessity and chance. To be free from the dread of guilt, paganism posits fate, which alleviates guilt at the price of freedom.

Judaism, which exemplifies for Kierkegaard the ethical culture, considers this too great a price to pay. It holds fast to the reality of guilt.

> Precisely by this fact [its dread of guilt] Judaism is further advanced than Hellenism. . . . [This] Judaism would not relinquish at any price for the sake of acquiring the lighter expressions of Hellenism: fate, luck, misfortune. [*CoD*, 93]

If the price of freedom is guilt, then so be it. Judaism is willing to pay the price. In the ethical culture there is the courage to accept the reality of guilt. There is no flight from freedom by positing the concept of fate, as in the aesthetic culture. What the ethicist values most is freedom, yet with freedom there comes guilt.

> There comes into being along with this *Ansich* of freedom another figure, guilt. This, like fate to the pagan, is the only thing he fears. . . . In the degree that he discovers freedom, in that same degree does the dread of guilt in the condition of possibility impend over him. Guilt only does he fear, for that is the one and only thing that can deprive him of freedom. [*CoD*, 97]

Ironically, however, such a preoccupation with guilt is itself a flight from freedom.

> The relation of freedom to guilt is dread, because freedom and guilt are still a possibility. But when freedom is thus with all its wishful passion staring at itself, and would keep guilt at a distance so that not a jot of it might be found in freedom, it is not able to refrain from staring at guilt, and this staring is the ambiguity of dread. [*CoD*, 97]

Here the ambiguity of dread is still present. The individual is both fascinated and repelléd by guilt. He lives in dread of being guilty, and yet he is fascinated by it. Guilt becomes the determinative category of his existence. The ethical culture has become preoccupied with guilt; it has replaced the dread of freedom with the dread of guilt. Out of the dread of freedom the ethical culture posits as its ultimate reality the law, obedience to which is thought to mean freedom from dread. But the consequence is that dread returns in the form of guilt. That dread is still present is betrayed by the compulsive quality of this concern for the law.

Of course, ethicism is not confined to Judaism. It is present wherever compulsive legalism arises out of the dread of freedom. Ethicism is present in Christendom—in Pelagianism, in the doctrine of "works righteousness," in certain forms of puritanism, and in the moralism of both fundamentalism and liberalism.

Law has been posited in the attempt to escape from dread. But, as in paganism, dread returns in the form of that which was posited as an escape from dread. That law does not accomplish its purpose is apparent in the continual repetition of the ritual sacrifice.

> The Jew has recourse to the sacrifice, but that is of no help to him, for what [alone can] ... help him would be that the relation of dread to guilt was annulled *(aufgehoben)* and a real relation posited. Inasmuch as this does not come to pass, the sacrifice becomes ambiguous, a fact which is expressed by its repetition. [*CoD*, 93]

Just as in paganism the persistence of dread was apparent in the compulsion to consult the oracle, so in Judaism the persistence of dread is apparent in the compulsion to repeat the sacrifice. The sacrificial acts of penance and self-punishment, whether outward or inward in character, cannot annul guilt. With this realization, a new concept is introduced: the concept of sin. Kierkegaard says, "Only with sin is atonement posited;

and its sacrifice is not repeated. . . . So long as the actual situation of sin is not posited, the sacrifice must be repeated" (*CoD*, 93). Only the concept of sin adequately takes into account both necessity and freedom. And only on such a basis is a restoration of the dialectic of selfhood possible.

The Religious Culture and the Concept of Sin

Only when the ethical notion of guilt is replaced by the ontological notion of sin is it possible to begin to come to terms with the problem of despair. The self is a relationship between necessity and possibility; this is its fundamental ontological structure. Despair is a disrelation in this relationship, and so it is also an ontological concept. Any attempt to understand the problem without reference to both poles of the ontological relationship is a misunderstanding which can never form the basis of a solution.

The aesthetic culture interprets despair in terms of fate and seeks to resolve the problem by means of the oracle. This approach is ultimately inadequate, however, for it fails to account for the existential reality of guilt. The ethical culture clings to the other pole of the dialectic. It interprets despair in terms of guilt and seeks to avoid despair by means of obedience to the law. But this approach proves inadequate too, for it fails to account for the inevitability of guilt. The ethical culture supposes the individual can avoid guilt. It assumes that despair originates in the individual's deliberate choice. But, as Kierkegaard points out, "the assumption of such a presupposition presents a greater difficulty than that which it would explain" (*CoD*, 97). On such an assumption it is utterly incomprehensible why anyone would choose despair. In order to explain sin one has to presuppose sin. Or, as Kierkegaard puts it, sin is the presupposition of sin, and every explanation is ultimately driven back to this enigma. Thus, just as the aesthetic culture founders upon the reality of guilt, so the ethical culture founders upon the reality of sin.

The Christian concept of original sin retains both of the

ontological elements in the dialectic of selfhood: necessity and possibility. Despair is both necessary and possible. The insight of paganism is preserved in the insistence upon the inevitability of despair, while the insight of Judaism is preserved in the insistence that it comes about in freedom. The emphasis upon individual responsibility arises from the basic presupposition of Spirit as the power of being; the inevitability of despair arises from the fact that dread is a necessary concomitant of freedom.

On the basis of such an interpretation Christianity proposes its own solution to the problem of despair. Paganism, on the basis of its aesthetic interpretation of despair as fate, seeks to resolve the problem by means of the oracle. Judaism, with its ethical interpretation of despair in terms of guilt, seeks its resolution in obedience to the law. And Christianity, with its ontological interpretation of despair as sin, proposes faith as the ultimate solution. I will not attempt to develop this concept here, as this is the concern of the last section of this essay. It is sufficient at this point to note that faith is a dialectical resolution of the problem of despair. It seeks to sustain an absolute relation to the Absolute (possibility), and a relative relation to the relative (necessity).

Again it must be noted that the religious solution is not confined to Christianity. Indeed a favorite paradigm of faith for Kierkegaard is Abraham. Nor is he oblivious to the failure of Christendom to remain true to its own peculiar insight. But he does maintain that the essence of Christianity is existence in faith, epitomized in the person of Jesus Christ.

5. Freud's Concept of Neurosis

The Nature of Neurosis

The central concern of this section is the problem of nonbeing with respect to man. In Part One human being was delineated in terms of the concept of the self, or the ego in Freud's terminology. This chapter will be concerned with Freud's interpretation of nonbeing, or the loss of selfhood, which he calls *neurosis*.

We have seen that Freud sought to interpret the phenomena of selfhood as a function of a basic energy or power which he called Libido. While at first this power of being was given an exclusively sexual interpretation, Freud increasingly came to see that it was but one aspect of a more fundamental life-instinct which he designated Eros. This life-instinct, then, was comprised of two broad categories: the sexual-instincts and the ego-instincts. In spite of his broadening understanding of the power of human being, Freud concentrated most of his research on the libidinal component of Eros. It was only in the latter part of his life that his interest turned increasingly to the ego-instincts.

Consequently, Freud's early theory construes selfhood as a function of the Libido. In the primal state of human being selfhood has not yet emerged. The primordial condition of the human being is simply that of an organism driven by certain instincts, the satisfaction of which is essential to the preservation of life. This stage of development is appropriately designated the *id*. In response to these drives there develops a secondary system of psychological processes which channel the energy of the organism into realistic means of gratification. This development marks the emergence of the self, for which Freud reserved the term *ego*.

Further studies convinced Freud, however, that this was only a rudimentary self. It was only the first stage of becoming. His study of the second class of instincts, the ego-instincts, led him to posit another stage in becoming a self. In order to become a self one must assume a relation to his self. That is, he must continually evaluate, censor, and control the behavior of the id with respect to another dimension of reality, namely, social reality. This can only be accomplished by means of an ego ideal, or *superego*, which is derived from the values of his society. There is thus a differentiating grade within the ego. Not only is the ego a relationship between the id and material reality, but it is also a relationship between the id and social reality. Nonbeing, then, must be a disrelation in this relationship.

Freud's early study of this phenomenon distinguished three types of nonbeing or neurosis: anxiety neurosis, hysterical neurosis, and obsessional neurosis. An examination of the aetiology of each will be undertaken later, but at this point I will simply describe the phenomena. Anxiety neurosis is characterized by an acute apprehension lest something dreadful occur. Freud writes, "Anxious expectation is the nuclear symptom of this neurosis" (*CP*, I, 80). It may take the form of hypochondria in which the dread relates to one's physical well-being. Or it may take the form of acute conscientiousness in which the dread relates to one's moral condition. This feeling of anxiety is accompanied by the appropriate organic disturbances, which may include palpitations of the heart, respiratory disturbance, excessive sweating, muscular tremor, ravenous hunger, diarrhea, vertigo, congestion, and paresthesia.

The second form of nonbeing, hysterical neurosis, is characterized by muscular debilitation of all kinds. In his description of the symptoms of this type of neurosis Freud lists the following:

> anaesthesias as well as neuralgias of the most varied kind, often of many years duration, contractures and paralyses, hysterical attacks and epileptoid convulsions which all observers had taken for genuine epilepsy, *petit-mal,* symptoms of the nature of tics, chronic vomiting and anorexia carried to the point of refusal of food, the most varied disturbances of vision, constantly recurring visual hallucinations—and the like. [*CP,* I, 25]

Finally, I will quote at length Freud's description of the third type of nonbeing, obsessional neurosis.

> The obsessional neurosis takes this form: the patient's mind is occupied with thoughts that do not really interest him, he feels impulses which seem alien to him, and he is impelled to perform actions which not only afford him no pleasure but from which he is powerless to desist. The thoughts (obsessions) may be meaningless in themselves . . . ; they are often absolutely silly. . . . The impulses which he perceives within him may seem to be of an equally childish and meaningless character; mostly, however, they consist of something terrifying, such as temptations to commit serious crimes, so that the patient not only repudiates them as alien, but flees from them in horror, and guards himself by prohibitions, precautions, and restrictions against the possibility of carrying them out. . . . The obsessive actions . . . are mostly repetitions and ceremonial elaborations of ordinary every-day performances . . . [such as] going to bed, washing, dressing, going for walks, etc. [*GIP,* 269-70]

In each type of neurosis there is a loss of selfhood. The ego has lost control and seems to be caught in the grip of some alien power. In the case of anxiety neurosis the ego is overwhelmed by a sense of dread or apprehension which can be almost totally debilitating. In the case of hysterical neurosis the debilitation of the ego is more physical in character. Here certain muscular paralyses occur for which there is no organic explanation, and yet the ego has lost control of that mechanism. In the case of obsessional neurosis the self is obsessed with an idea which expresses itself in some compulsive activity which the ego is helpless to control.

Along with Charcot and Janet, Freud was among the first to show that these maladies are of psychological and not organic origin. He carefully delineated the differences between organic and hysterical paralyses in an essay in 1893 (*CP*, I, 42-58). The next year he set forth the justification for distinguishing the anxiety neurosis from neurasthenia, an organic condition (*CP*, I, 76-106); a year later he extended this distinction to obsessional neurosis (*CP*, I, 128-37). The loss of selfhood in each case, then, is essentially a psychological phenomenon and not an organic one.

The question of the aetiology of this sickness of selfhood and the factors which determine the form the neurosis will take must now be examined. But some attention should be given first to the mode of investigation which Freud employed in his research into the problem of nonbeing. Freud clearly broke with the prevailing rationalistic psychology of his day—a psychology which sought to understand human behavior exclusively in terms of the activity of a conscious rational ego. Freud was aware of an unconscious or depth dimension of the self. The id, to be sure, is unconscious, but there is also an unconscious aspect of the ego which exercises a censorship or repression which is wholly below the threshold of consciousness. Here in this "forgotten" material lies the answer to the puzzling phenomena of neurosis. What method is appropriate for ferreting out this kind of material? Certainly one cannot rely on the conscious recollection of the patient. Some method must be devised which can disclose the contents of the unconscious.

At first Freud tried hypnosis to induce the patient to discuss the experiences coincident with the genesis of the neurosis. This method was highly successful in disclosing the material which was required to understand the neurotic phenomena. But for therapeutic reasons Freud soon dropped the hypnotic method of investigation in favor of what he called "free association."[1] In an essay entitled "Freud's Psycho-analytic Method" he described this method in the third person.

> In order to secure these ideas and associations he asks the patient to 'let himself go' in what he says, 'as you would do in a conversation which leads you "from cabbages to kings" '. . . . He admonishes them to relate everything that passes through their minds, even if they think it unimportant or irrelevant or nonsensical; he lays special stress on their not omitting any thought or idea from their story because to relate it might be embarrassing or painful to them. In the task of collecting this material of otherwise neglected ideas Freud made the observations which became the determining factors of his entire theory. [*CP*, I, 266-67]

On the basis of these disclosures Freud was able to develop a theory concerning the origin and nature of the neurotic phenomena.

The Concept of Repression

Anxiety: The Presupposition of Repression

As a student of Joseph Breuer, Freud's attention was drawn to the role which painful memories of past experiences play in hysteria. Breuer's thesis was that forgotten memories continue to influence the conscious behavior of the individual. In one of his earliest papers, "The Defence Neuro-Psychoses" (1894; *CP*, I, 61-74), Freud sought to extend this thesis to several of the more common neurotic manifestations. He suggested the fol-

---

1. The therapeutic considerations which influenced Freud's method of investigation will be explored fully in Part Three.

lowing aetiology. The individual enjoys good mental health until the ego is confronted with an experience or feeling which causes so much emotional distress that it is utterly intolerable. To escape from this painful experience the ego "forgets" it. But this kind of forgetting does not succeed. The anxiety aroused by the event manifests itself in various pathological symptoms such as hysteria, obsessions, and phobias. In the case of hysteria, the intolerable idea is rendered innocuous by transmuting the Libido associated with it into some bodily form of expression. Alternatively, this Libido may be invested in other ideas which are not unacceptable, in which case these inappropriate ideas become obsessions. Or the energy may remain unattached creating a vague sense of misapprehension or "free-floating" anxiety, which in turn seeks to objectify itself, so to speak. It may then attach itself to any object and become manifest as one kind of phobia or another.

Further investigation by means of the psychoanalytic method convinced Freud that the conditions which predispose the individual to neurotic illness arise from a traumatic experience in early childhood. From the content of his patient's disclosures he concluded that this early trauma was sexual in nature.

> [Such] premature sexual stimulation produces little or no effect at the time, but a mental impression of it is retained. Later, at puberty, when the sexual organs have developed . . . , this unconscious mental impression is somehow or other reawakened . . . [to] exercise a power which was entirely lacking when the experience itself took place; *the memory will produce the same result* as if it were an actual event. We have, so to speak, *the subsequent effect of a sexual trauma.* [*CP*, I, 151]

Subsequent study led Freud to turn away from this emphasis on a traumatic sexual event. He confessed that he had overestimated the frequency of these infantile sexual traumas. He found "many a phantasy of seduction . . . to be an attempt at defense against the memory of sexual activities practiced by the child himself" (*CP*, I, 276). Furthermore,

> investigation into the mental life of normal persons then yielded the unexpected discovery that their infantile history in regard to sexual matters was not necessarily different in essentials from that of the neurotic. . . . The important thing, therefore, was evidently not the sexual stimulation that the person had experienced during childhood; what mattered was, above all, how he had reacted to these experiences. [*CP*, I, 279]

In *Three Contributions to the Theory of Sex* (1905) Freud set forth his theory of libidinal development, a process which goes through several stages. The auto-erotism of infancy gives way to the Oedipal period when the Libido is invested in the parental object. Social taboo forces the suppression of the libidinal drive for a time called the latency period. During this period the superego structures are developed. Finally, during puberty the mastery of the Libido is completed, partially through sublimation and partially through the subordination of the Libido to the reproductive end. Neurosis results from a breakdown in this normal development—from the inadequate mastery of the Libido and the consequent necessity to repress it. Hence, the concept of *repression* holds the key to understanding the origin of neurosis.

It was to this phenomenon that Freud next turned his attention. Publishing his conclusions in an essay in 1915 (*CP*, IV, 84-97), Freud observed that repression is a mode of flight from an internal threat. If the ego were threatened from an external stimulus, flight would be an appropriate response. But one cannot flee from an internal threat, so repression is the ego's way of dealing with it. "Later on," he added "rejection based on judgement (condemnation) will be a good weapon against the impulse. Repression is a preliminary phase of condemnation, something between flight and condemnation" (*CP*, IV, 84).

Actually, this phenomenon is not properly referred to as repression. It is a kind of prototype of repression. Repression proper is an entirely unconscious process, whereas this initial rejection of the instinct is motivated by an external taboo and is primarily a conscious process. This primal repression, however, does not destroy the instinct.

> We may imagine that what is repressed exercises a continuous straining in the direction of consciousness, so that the balance has to be kept by means of a steady counterpressure. A constant expenditure of energy, therefore, is entailed in maintaining the repression. [*CP*, IV, 90]

In fact, the repressed instinct gains in strength due to the accumulation of Libido. In order to maintain the primal repression other defense mechanisms are necessary. Perhaps the earliest defense is that of *regression*. In the face of the parental taboo, the ego regresses to a pre-Oedipal stage in which the libidinal drive is auto-erotic and the Oedipal object-choice is relatively dormant. During this latency period the ego develops yet another line of defense. A reaction-formation develops in which a counteractant unconscious force is created to maintain the repression. This, of course, is the superego. Thus, the conflict is no longer between the Libido and an external taboo, but becomes a conflict between the Libido and an internalized taboo which functions largely unconsciously. The process whereby the instinct is rejected from consciousness may now properly be called repression. Ultimately, the ego must develop the capacity to channel the Libido into socially acceptable modes of expression rather than deny it expression through repression. This process is called *sublimation*.

But why should an instinctual impulse be rejected? According to the pleasure/pain principle the satisfaction of the instinctual impulse would have to produce pain to necessitate its rejection. The aim of an instinctual drive, however, is always pleasure. Consequently, Freud assumes that another factor has been introduced which creates an ambivalent reaction to the instinctual drive. That factor, of course, is the social taboo. The instinctual drive whose gratification results in pleasure encounters a social taboo, the violation of which would result in punishment or rejection. As a result, the instinct which would normally produce pleasure induces anxiety.

This anxiety is essentially a "separation anxiety" which has roots reaching back to the traumatic experience of birth in which the child is separated from the prenatal idyllic situation where there was immediate gratification of all its needs. Thus, anxiety is a danger signal, a response to a situation in which the initial threat of separation is experienced once again. This separation anxiety is manifested in various ways throughout the course of the individual's development. Perhaps the earliest form is the dread of the loss of parental love. Later it is generalized into a dread of social rejection, internalized as a dread of the superego and ontologized as a dread of death—the supreme form of separation (*PoA*, 76).

Essentially anxiety is objectless. The instinctual drive is not the object of anxiety. "Instinctual demands," Freud points out, "become an (internal) danger only because of the fact that their gratification would bring about an external danger" (*PoA*, 116). It is simply that certain situations evoke the same psychic response which was first experienced in birth—a vague sense of apprehension. "Anxiety is undeniably related to expectation; one feels anxiety *lest* something occur. It is endowed with a certain character of indefiniteness and objectlessness; correct usage even changes its name when it has found an object, and in that case speaks instead of *dread*" (*PoA*, 112). The occasion of helplessness which instigates this subsequent anxiety is evoked by the prohibition of the basic life-instinct, the Libido. Confronted by this social taboo, the old anxiety, which was first experienced in the primal situation of birth, emerges.

"Anxiety is the reaction to a situation of danger," Freud writes, "and it is circumvented by the ego's doing something to avoid the situation or retreat from it. One might say, then, that symptoms are created in order to avoid the development of anxiety" (*PoA,* 65). In the face of an anxiety-producing situation, the neurotic response is flight or regression to a more primitive mode of handling the situation. If the flight is to the latency period, reaction-formation is the mode of defense, and *obsessional neurosis* results. The individual becomes obsessed with ideas which seek to counteract the idea which evoked the anxiety. A similar mechanism is what Freud calls "undoing." Here the ego seeks to nullify an impulse or action which threatens his security by means of another compensating action. In either case the defense is maintained with a compulsion born of dread.

If the regression proceeds back into the Oedipal period, *hysterical neurosis* results. Repression is the characteristic mode of defense for it is derived from that period of development. Self-punishment replaces atonement as the characteristic defense against the impulse or idea which precipitated the anxiety.

Finally, if the regression is even more pronounced and the flight proceeds back into the auto-erotic period of development, *anxiety neurosis* is the consequence. The response is neither compulsive atonement nor punishment, but a debilitating dread which can lead to a suspension of all activity. Freud calls this mechanism "isolation." Here the ego is terrified into inactivity by the threatening idea or impulse. It interposes a period in which nothing more is allowed to happen, nothing is remembered, no perception is registered, no action permitted.[2]

Freud also sought to account for the degree of regression which takes place in the various types of neurosis. That is, he sought to understand why the regression proceeds to one level in some cases and to another in others, and he found the answer in his concept of *fixation.* He theorized that the process of mastering the libidinal impulse is

2. A more detailed discussion of the defense mechanisms may be found in *The Problem of Anxiety,* pp. 46-55.

not always carried out without a hitch, so that the function as a whole is not always subjected to progressive modification. Should any component of it remain arrested at an earlier phase there results what is known as a 'fixation-point', to which the function can regress if external hardships give rise to illness. [*CP*, II, 123]

Thus, the predisposition to a particular neurosis is related to the arrested development of the ego at a specific stage. Later, the frustration of the individual's characteristic way of dealing with the libidinal impulse results in regression to that stage in the development of the ego at which particular difficulty was experienced—in short, to the last successful stage in the mastery of the Libido.

It should be apparent that such neurotic defenses are not ultimately successful. They do not resolve the problem once and for all. Freud says of repression, "After the first act of repression there follows a lengthy or never-ending epilogue: the struggle against the instinctual impulse is continued in the struggle against the symptom" (*PoA*, 25). And what he says of repression is true of all the other ego defenses. Once the symptom formation is created, once the pattern of defense has been established, the recurrence of the instinctual threat is dealt with automatically in the same fashion. The neurotic pattern of behavior becomes repetitious. The ego has sacrificed that portion of its sovereignty and to that extent has lost its selfhood.

Guilt: The Consequence of Repression

We have seen how, in the social context, the libidinal impulse evokes a sense of anxiety which motivates the repression of this impulse followed by certain other defense mechanisms intended to sustain the repression. Chief among these in the normal psychic development is reaction-formation, for by means of it the superego is developed. But with this development arises a sense of guilt. "The tension between the strict superego and the subordinate ego we call the sense of guilt; it manifests itself as the need for punishment" (*C&D*, 77). In the normal individual this sense of guilt is relieved by conforming to the normative demands of the superego.

But this is too facile an interpretation of guilt. There are too many instances in which guilt is experienced where there is no objective culpability. In compulsive or obsessional neurosis, for example, the individual is possessed with an overwhelming sense of guilt. And even in cases where the sense of guilt is lacking Freud notes, "the ego has saved itself from the perception of guilt by means of a new series of self-punitive symptoms, atonements, and restrictions" (*PoA*, 51). This is an ambiguous guilt. "The ego which knows on the one hand that it is innocent has on the other to experience a feeling of guilt and to carry a feeling of responsibility which it is unable to account for" (*PoA*, 51). Furthermore, Freud suspected that many criminal acts are motivated by a preexistent guilt feeling, a sense of guilt which exists prior to the transgression. Regarding such cases he wrote,

> The analytic work then afforded the surprising conclusion that such deeds are done precisely *because* they are forbidden and because by carrying them out the doer enjoys a sense of mental relief. He suffered from an oppressive feeling of guilt, of which he did not know the origin, and after he had committed a misdeed the oppression was mitigated. The sense of guilt was at least in some way accounted for. [*CP*, IV, 342]

But it is not just the criminal who experiences this perverse sense of guilt. Ironically, it is often the most "saintly" individual who has the deepest sense of guilt. "The more righteous a man is, the stricter and more suspicious will his conscience be, so that ultimately it is precisely those people who have carried holiness farthest who reproach themselves with the deepest sinfulness" (*C&D*, 80).

Obviously, the naive explanation of guilt does not suffice;

namely, that the sense of guilt arises from an action for which one is objectively culpable. However, neither does the more subtle explanation that the guilt feeling arises when the individual becomes aware of his *intention* to do evil. "In both cases," Freud points out, "one is presupposing that wickedness has already been recognized as reprehensible" (*C&D*, 77). But how is this judgment arrived at? Freud rejected the hypothesis of an inherent moral capacity for distinguishing good from evil. That which we call evil is often precisely the thing that we desire most, that which would give us pleasure. Evidently there is some external influence at work here, or men would obey their immediate impulses—and without guilt.

Freud claimed that the external authority of good and evil is society. The motivation for obeying this authority stems from the contingency of man, his dependence upon others for his security. He dreads the loss of the love and acceptance of others. If he loses this he feels helpless, threatened, and anxious. "What is bad is, therefore, to begin with, whatever causes one to be threatened with a loss of love; because of the dread of this loss, one must desist from it" (*C&D*, 78). Originally this is a dread of the loss of parental love, due to the child's contingent relationship with his parents. But as the child matures the larger human community supplants the parents as a source of security and moral authority. In early childhood, the dread is only the dread of discovery and guilt applies only to wrong deeds actually committed. Many people never get beyond this stage of development. "Such people habitually permit themselves to do any bad deed that procures them something they want, if only they are sure that no authority will discover it or make them suffer for it; their anxiety relates only to the possibility of detection" (*C&D*, 79). But when the authority has been internalized through the creation of a superego the dread of discovery is supplanted by the dread of the impulse itself, and guilt is now experienced in relation not only to the deed, or even to the conscious intention, but also in relation to the impulse itself. The difference between doing evil and wishing it no longer prevails, for "nothing is hidden from the superego, not even thoughts" (*C&D*, 79).

Thus, there are two sources of guilt feelings: the external, objective authority of society, and the internal, subjective authority of the superego. The former motivates the renunciation of instinctual gratification; the latter demands punishment in addition to renunciation. Originally the dread of the external authority results in instinct renunciation; one gives up certain pleasures in order not to jeopardize his social security. Having done so, he should be done with guilt. But where the superego exists renunciation does not suffice. The instinctual desire persists and cannot be hidden from the superego. So, in spite of renunciations, the individual feels guilty. Indeed, as we have already observed, the more righteous a man is, the more profound the guilt consciousness. Freud even suggests that instinct renunciation may lead to a heightened sense of guilt, due to the intensification of pent-up desire.

> In the beginning conscience (more correctly, the anxiety which later became conscience) was the cause of instinctual renunciation, but later this relation is reversed. Every renunciation then becomes a dynamic fount of conscience; every fresh abandonment of gratification increases its severity and intolerance. . . . Renunciation (externally imposed) gives rise to conscience, which then demands further renunciations. [*C&D*, 83]

The problem of guilt becomes more complex when we take into account the phenomenon of aggression. Freud claims that aggression arises from the frustration of libidinal desire. "The thwarting of the erotic gratification provokes an excess of aggressiveness against the person who interfered with the gratification, and then this tendency to aggression in its turn has to be suppressed" (*C&D*, 96). Thus the dynamics of guilt are as follows: The frustration of the libidinal drive produces aggression against the source of the taboo. The aggression, in turn, must be repressed for it threatens the individual's social security. The internalized authority, the superego, accomplishes this by turning the aggression back upon the ego in the form of guilt or the sense of the need for punishment. Freud concludes:

> Guilt is the expression of the conflict of ambivalence, the eternal struggle between Eros and the destructive or death instinct. This conflict is engendered as soon as man is confronted with the task of living with his fellows; as long as he knows no other form of life in common but that of the family, it must express itself in the Oedipus complex, cause the development of conscience and create the first feelings of guilt. When mankind tries to institute wider forms of communal life, the same conflict continues to arise—in forms derived from the past—and intensified so that a further reinforcement of the sense of guilt results. [*C&D*, 88-89]

Neurosis and Psychosis

Thus far we have been concerned with an examination of the aetiology of the neuroses. We have seen a kind of gradation or potentiation of neurosis which is a function of the degree of regression to which the ego must go in order to handle the anxiety evoked by the libidinal impulse as it confronts the internalized social prohibition of the superego. This potentiation proceeds from obsessional neurosis to hysterical neurosis to anxiety neurosis. There is here a progressive loss of selfhood. The initial response of the individual to the anxiety occasioned by the conflict between the libidinal desire and the social taboo is the same: the Libido is withdrawn from the external object of its desire by means of the mechanism of repression. The distinction between the normal individual and the neurotic depends on the secondary response. Normally the Libido is sublimated into socially acceptable modes of expression. But if the capacity for sublimation has not been adequately developed, or if the repressive force of the superego is excessive, other less satisfactory ways of dealing with the situation may result.

In the case of obsessional neurosis contact with reality is sustained, but the libidinal threat is met by an anticathexis or reaction-formation whereby the ego becomes preoccupied with a substitute idea or action which is clearly intended to negate the original intolerable idea or impulse. The consequent compulsion to sustain the negating function of this obsession is apparent.

The dynamics of hysterical neurosis are quite similar, but here the reaction is less subtle. The libidinal threat is met with the punishment of the offending agent of libidinal expression, and physical incapacitation results. Nevertheless, the Libido finds some kind of expression, albeit in a crippled form, and the ego's relation to reality is more tenuous than ever.

In anxiety neurosis this relationship is even more attenuated. Here the Libido remains relatively uninvested in external reality. A vague, objectless, free-floating anxiety results. However, so long as there is any contact with external reality, some attempt to resolve the distressing situation is made. The free-floating anxiety is directed toward some innocuous object which results in various irrational phobias.

> The fugitive cathexis attached itself to a substitutive idea which, on the one hand, was connected by association with the rejected idea, and, on the other, escaped repression by reason of its remoteness from that idea. . . . The substitutive idea now plays the part of an anti-cathexis for the (conscious) system . . . by securing that system against an emergence into consciousness of the repressed idea; on the other hand, it is, or acts as if it were, the point at which the anxiety-affect, which is now all the more uncontrollable, may break out and be discharged. [*CP*, IV, 115]

As a result, repression must now be directed to the task of

inhibiting the outbreak of anxiety concerning the substitute idea. All kinds of defenses against encountering the object of the phobia now develop.

Each of these methods of handling Libido is crippling to the ego for each requires an inordinate expenditure of energy in avoiding the phobic object, sustaining the hysterical paralysis, or repeating the compulsive atonement. In each case the attempt to avoid anxiety has failed, for it is present in each in disguise.

Although there is an incipient nonbeing present in each of the above types of neurosis, still selfhood of some sort is sustained because the ego retains some kind of relationship to reality. But Freud was aware of that much more pernicious kind of nonbeing called psychosis or schizophrenia. His psychoanalytic method of investigation proved less effective in the study of psychosis, for reasons I will soon note, but he did seek to extend his theory to this phenomenon as well.

Again the initial response to the libidinal threat is the same. In the face of the anxiety occasioned by the conflict between the Libido and the social taboo, the Libido is withdrawn from the external object of desire. But, whereas in the transference neuroses the Libido was transferred to another object, however inadequate, Freud noted that

> in schizophrenia . . . we have been obliged to assume that after the process of repression the withdrawn libido does not seek a new object, but retreats into the ego; that is to say, that here the object-cathexes are given up and a primitive objectless condition of narcissism is re-established. [*CP*, IV, 128]

Freud illustrated this in his paper on melancholia. The predisposition to melancholia lies in a narcissistic type of object-choice. That is to say, the original investment of the Libido in a love-object was not a genuine erotic cathexis but a narcissistic one. The apparent love relation was actually merely a form of self-love. Thus, when the relationship was vitiated through some disappointment in the love-object, "the result was not the normal one of withdrawal of the Libido from this object and transference of it to a new one. ... The free Libido was withdrawn into the ego and not directed to another object" (*CP*, IV, 159). The Libido was invested in the ego as the substitute for the lost object. Thus melancholia is "the process of regression from narcissistic object-choice to narcissism" (*CP*, IV, 161). The hostility which the individual would normally experience toward the former object of love is now directed upon the ego, due to this narcissistic identification. All kinds of self-punishment, even suicide, ensue.

Curiously, there is a reverse side to this phenomenon, the manic side. The dynamics here are the same, only in the manic phase the narcissistic love has triumphed, temporarily, over the narcissistic hate which resulted from the identification of the ego with its lost love-object. Both tendencies persist in continual tension, first one dominating the syndrome, and then the other.

In summary then, the difference between neurosis and psychosis is this: "Neurosis is the result of a conflict between the ego and its id, whereas psychosis is the analogous outcome of a similar disturbance in the relation between the ego and its environment" (*CP*, II, 251). Both result from the frustration of the id-impulse.

> The pathogenic effect depends on whether, in the tension of such a conflict, the ego remains true in its allegiance to the outer world and endeavours to subjugate the *id*, or whether it allows itself to be overwhelmed by the *id* and thus torn away from reality. [*CP*, II, 253]

If the ego allies itself with reality and suppresses the id, neurosis results. If it allies itself with the id and withdraws from reality, psychosis results. In schizophrenia the ego creates its own reality. It creates delusional systems, hallucinations, and—in short—it remodels reality to suit its own psychic needs.

In severe catatonic schizophrenia, the relation with reality is completely severed.

The perversity of this form of nonbeing is apparent when compared with the normal and the neurotic forms of guilt. A progressive potentiation of the sense of guilt can be discerned throughout the various neuroses and psychoses. Guilt is present, of course, in the normal individual and he takes realistic steps to avoid or reduce the intensity of such a painful perception through obedience to the mores of society. Here guilt is clearly perceptible to consciousness, and we commonly speak of a "consciousness of guilt." But in many of the neurotic conditions the individual is wholly unconscious of any guilt. Here we speak of an "unconscious sense of guilt."

In obsessional neurosis guilt is clearly expressed in the compulsive atonements with which it is constantly preoccupied. "The sense of guilt expresses itself loudly but cannot justify itself to the ego. Consequently the patient's ego rebels against this imputation of guilt and seeks the physician's support in repudiating it" (*E&I*, 73). In hysterical neurosis guilt is more obscure because "the ego contents itself with keeping at a distance the material to which the sense of guilt refers" (*E&I*, 75). But the presence of guilt is apparent from the exaggerated punishments which the ego inflicts upon itself. The presence of guilt in anxiety neurosis is detached in the pervasive paranoia with which the self confronts his world.

But in schizophrenia the potentiation of guilt reaches its extremity, as Freud points out in his study of melancholia. "In melancholia, the impression that the super-ego has obtained a hold upon consciousness is even stronger. But in this case the ego ventures no objection; it admits the guilt and submits to the punishment" (*E&I*, 74). Freud concludes:

> The destructive component [has] entrenched itself in the super-ego and turned against the ego. What is now holding sway in the super-ego is, as it were, a pure culture of the death-instinct, and in fact it often enough succeeds in

driving the ego into death, if the latter does not protect itself from the tyrant in time by a revulsion into mania. [*E&I*, 77]

The condition of some individuals gets worse when any encouraging word is given concerning the progress they are making. Such people react inversely to the progress of the treatment. The nearer they come to the core of their problem, the more stubbornly they resist. "There is something in these people that sets itself against their recovery and dreads its approach as though it were a danger" (*E&I*, 70-71). Freud reasons,

> We are dealing with what may be called a 'moral' factor, a sense of guilt, which is finding atonement in the illness and is refusing to give up the penalty of suffering. . . . But as far as the patient is concerned this sense of guilt is dumb; it does not tell him he is guilty; he does not feel guilty, he simply feels ill. This sense of guilt expresses itself only as a resistance to recovery which it is extremely difficult to overcome. [*E&I*, 71-72]

This sickness is therefore a pernicious thing which wills its own continuation. It is present in a mild form in even the so-called normal individual, and its ultimate significance is seen in the extreme manifestation of manic-depressive psychosis in which the individual wills his own destruction.

The Neurotic Culture

Freud's interpretation of man presupposes a cultural context. It is culture which requires instinct renunciation. It is culture which determines the character of the superego. It is culture which gives rise to the various neurotic defenses. But why? What is the function of culture? What is its origin and purpose? Freud increasingly turned his attention to the problem of culture. He suggested that culture has two fundamental functions, "namely, that of protecting humanity against nature and of regulating the relations of human beings among themselves" (*C&D*, 33). While the primary purpose of culture is to provide a defense against the threat which nature poses, its institution creates a secondary purpose, that of regulating the social relations of men. To protect himself against nature man was forced into social existence, but social existence necessitates the subordination of individual desires to the requirements of the group, and this in turn requires a certain amount of coercion and restriction.

In the primal situation man finds himself in the threatening context of nature. He experiences nature as an overwhelming complex of hostile forces which threaten his very existence. Even the advantages of the mutual physical protection which the group provides do not begin to overcome the anxiety which this human predicament evokes. It is the function of culture to augment this defense against the threat of nature. The first step in this defense is the humanization of nature.

> Nothing can be made of impersonal forces and fates; they remain eternally remote. But . . . if everywhere in nature we have about us beings who resemble those of our own environment, then . . . we can deal psychically with our frantic anxiety. We . . . can have recourse to the same methods against these violent supermen of the beyond that we make use of in our own community; we can try to exorcise them, to appease them, to bribe them, and so to rob them of part of their power by thus influencing them. [*FoI*, 25]

The humanization of nature is accomplished in accordance with the pattern already established in infancy. In the child's helplessness he depends upon his parents, especially his father, whom he fears and yet in whose protection he finds security. "Similarly man makes the forces of nature not simply in the image of men with whom he can associate as his equals—that would not do justice to the overpowering impression they make on him—but he gives them the characteristics of the father, makes them into gods" (*FoI*, 26-27). But this cultural defense does not quite satisfy. The orderliness and regularity of nature is observed by man; nature seems to possess an inward necessity over which even the gods have no power. If the gods create fate, then they are indeed inscrutable. In the Greek notion of fate there lingers the suspicion that the perplexity and helplessness of man cannot be remedied. "The most gifted people of the ancient world dimly surmised that above the gods stands Destiny and that the gods themselves have their destinies" (*FoI*, 28). Nature or Fate has an independent status which transcends the gods. The Greek religion is seen to be inadequate. The powers of the gods have become limited, their jurisdiction increasingly circumscribed to the realm of ethics. They retain their dual function, but the emphasis has shifted from nature to society. The chief function of the gods now becomes ethical in character.

Freud suggests that the ethical response to the human predicament culminates in the Jewish religion, where "fate is felt to be a substitute for the agency of the parents: adversity means that one is no longer loved by this highest power of all, and, threatened by this loss of love, one humbles himself again before the representative of the parents" (*C&D*, 81). The focus of anxiety, we note, has shifted from the dread of death to the dread of rejection. Here the response to adversity is guilt and remorse. The hostility is internalized. Contrast this response with that of the more primitive religion. In a primitive culture, Freud says, the savage belabors his fetish in response to misfortune, whereas in an ethical culture the individual punishes himself. He continues:

> As long as things go well with a man, his conscience is lenient and lets the ego do all kinds of things; when some calamity befalls, he holds an inquisition within, discovers his sin, heightens the standards of his conscience, imposes abstinences on himself and punishes himself with penances. [*C&D*, 80]

Nor will the individual relinquish this burden of guilt. All the adversity which befell the people of Israel never shook them in their belief that they were God's chosen people. They never doubted his power or his justice; "they proceeded instead to bring their prophets into the world to declare their sinfulness to them and out of their sense of guilt they constructed the stringent commandments of their priestly religion" (*C&D*, 81).

The problem of an ethical culture, therefore, is progressive. Externally imposed prohibitions give rise to conscience, and conscience demands increased prohibitions. The tolerance of this cumulative instinctual renunciation proves increasingly difficult. Hostility toward the source of the prohibition continually threatens to break out, and this hostility in turn must be suppressed. To accomplish this task society erects its cultural ideal, which it institutionalizes and defends with every possible sanction at its command. The ethical requirements of culture are fortified by the claim to divine origin and thus subject to divine enforcement. Society's stringent taboos are enunciated at the weakest points of its defense. The social ethic, in short, is a kind of cultural reaction-formation, a cultural superego. if you please.

> The super-ego of any given epoch of civilization originates in the same way as that of an individual; it is based on the impression left behind them by great leading personalities, men of outstanding force of mind, or men in whom some one human tendency has developed in unusual strength and purity. [*C&D*, 100]

The characteristic hostility toward the superego may find expression in the persecution and even the murder of such formative personalities, but, ironically, the ethical residue is thereby strengthened by the consequent guilt. Freud hypothesized that the origin of this persistent sense of guilt stems from the primal murder of the tribal father—in the case of the Jewish people, Moses—to whom are attributed all the ethical precepts of the culture. Expiation of the guilt is sought in per-

sistent ethical striving to fulfill the father's will. Freud pro-
posed this theory of the origin of culture in *Totem and Taboo*
(1913), and developed it with respect to the Jewish culture in
Moses and Monotheism (1939). Whether or not the historicity
of the primal murder can be defended, the psychological validity of the interpretation is commensurate with his theory of
the self. That is to say, the ethical response of culture stems
from the universal ambivalence toward the father. The guilt
which it experiences over the hostility toward the father is
compensated for by a compulsive obedience to his ethical
commandments. The guilt response of culture is simply the
cosmic projection of the Oedipal relationship.

In the same work, Freud notes that Christianity represents
an attempt to overcome this guilt response of culture. Freud
attributes the Christian religion to St. Paul, suggesting that he
"seized upon this feeling of guilt and correctly traced it back
to its primeval source. This he called original sin; it was a crime
against God that could be expiated only through death"
(*M&M*, 109). Freud claims that the truth which Paul discerned
was that we are guilty because we have killed the Father-God.
To be sure, Paul never so designates the original crime; instead,
he employs the "shadowy concept of original sin." But, considering the enormity of the crime, "it is quite clear to us why
he could grasp this truth in no other form but in the delusional
guise of the glad tidings: 'We have been delivered from all guilt
since one of us laid down his life to expiate our guilt' " (*M&M*,
174). Freud reasons that the expiation of guilt through the
sacrifice of the sinless *Son* of God can only mean that the
original crime was the murder of the *Father*. Thus, the doctrine of original sin and salvation through the sacrificial death
of Jesus Christ became the basis of the new religion. The religion of the Son replaced the religion of the Father. Paul's
success "was certainly mainly due to the fact that through the
idea of salvation he laid the ghost of the feeling of guilt"
(*M&M*, 112). It is interesting to note the way in which the new
religion came to terms with the perennial ambivalence of the

son toward the father. In Judaism the children of God remain
his children, and guilt is atoned for by intense moral obedience, while in Christianity the Father is in effect overthrown,
and his place usurped by the Son. In place of guilt-motivated
moral obedience, there is the confession of sin and the acceptance of the atoning death of Christ. "Why the Jews were
unable to participate in the progress which this confession to
the murder of God betokened," Freud observes, "might well
be the subject of a special investigation. Through this they
have, so to speak, shouldered a tragic guilt" (*M&M*, 176).

This whole religious development—from primitive animism
to Greek fatalism to Jewish moralism to Christianity—constitutes for Freud an immature if not neurotic way of meeting
the human predicament. The obsession with guilt, the compulsive morality, the construction of the illusory reality may
be expedient ways for culture to deal with the anxious predicament of man, but they are essentially neurotic. To be sure,
"the true believer is in a high degree protected against the
danger of certain neurotic afflictions; by accepting the universal neurosis he is spared the task of forming a personal
neurosis" (*FoI*, 79). But just as the child must outgrow the
neurotic phases of his development, so our culture must abandon its primitive defenses which have become neurotic. As we
have earlier noted, Freud calls for a culture founded on reason,
a culture in which reason will accomplish what fate and guilt
cannot. Of course, necessity looms over man with a stubborn-
ness he cannot escape. But instead of responding to it in guilt,
or through the creation of an illusory utopia beyond this
world, man will learn to do all that he can by means of reason
within the limitations of necessity, and to endure the rest with
resignation (*FoI*, 89). This will require, of course, an "education to reality," as Freud terms it, in place of the flight from
reality which now characterizes our culture.

6. Interpolation: The Loss of Selfhood

The Sickness of the Self

The sickness of the self, as Kierkegaard reminds us, has been approached from all kinds of perspectives: fear, condemnation, pity, compassion, and objectivity. It has been variously attributed to physical causes, demon possession, the wrath of God, and moral guilt. And it has been treated by isolation, exhortation, torture, punishment, and pills. For most of the history of human existence this sickness has remained an enigma. In some measure it is still so, but much of the mystery has been clarified within the last one hundred years. The pioneers in this endeavor were Kierkegaard and Freud. The one—apparently a sufferer from the soul-sickness himself—gained his insight from self-analysis; the other, from a lifetime of clinical experience. To be sure, each interprets the phenomena from radically different perspectives. Freud approaches the sickness psychosomatically, i.e. he treats it as a libidinal phenomenon. Kierkegaard's approach, on the other hand, is pneumatic, which is to say, he treats it as a spiritual phenomenon. Each interprets the sickness by means of his central category, but this does not mean that the two interpretations are mutually exclusive. It is the thesis of this study that the differences are perspectival and that the two views are supplementary. In this section of my essay I intend to interpolate between the two perspectives on the sickness of the self.

The basis for this interpolation is to be found in Kierkegaard's understanding of man as a synthesis of body and soul which is brought about in freedom. Or, put another way, man is a psychosomatic synthesis sustained by means of the pneuma or Spirit. Consequently, the human phenomenon may be interpreted from any of the following perspectives. Man may be viewed as a somatic, psychic, or pneumatic phenomenon, and each is valid—within limits. Selfhood may be lost "somatic-psychically," or it may be lost "pneumatically." The sickness of the self *is* a libidinal phenomenon, but it is also— and simultaneously—a spiritual phenomenon. It is somatic, as Freud's first theory of neurosis discerned; it is psychological, as his later theory perceives; but, as Kierkegaard insists, it is also pneumatic.

The essence of human being is selfhood. That is to say, selfhood is the mode of being peculiar to men. As we have seen in Part One, Kierkegaard and Freud have a similar understanding of what constitutes selfhood, though they approach the matter from widely differing standpoints. Beginning from a naturalistic orientation, Freud arrives at the conclusion that the self or ego is a functional relationship between the Libido and reality—a reality both material and social. Kierkegaard, stressing the historical character of human existence, comes to the conclusion that the self is a relation which relates its immediate self to a transcendent ideal. In spite of their different perspectives, they essentially agree that selfhood consists in a relationship in which the self responsibly relates itself to a reality which transcends the individual. Human being, therefore, is essentially a relationship; conversely, nonbeing is a disrelation in the relationship. Kierkegaard terms this disrelationship *despair* and considers it to be a sickness unto death, a sickness which destroys the self. Freud's term for nonbeing is *neurosis,* which he also understands to be a fatal sickness of the self. It is the triumph of the death-instinct in man.

Now, obviously, in his primal state man is not yet a self. He is not yet self-determined, but is determined by nature. At this stage man is what Freud refers to as an id. Like the animals he is entirely motivated by instinctual drives. Certainly this is not yet the human mode of being. According to the concept of *human* being which I have just enunciated, this is nonbeing. And yet, selfhood is latently present even in the primal state of man. If it were not, Kierkegaard points out, an individual could never become a self. This nonbeing which is nonetheless a being is what Kierkegaard calls the state of innocence. Here being is not present as being, but only as a potentiality to be actualized. However, this absence of being is not the nonbeing of guilt, a nonbeing in which being is present *in potentia*. Being, or selfhood, is not given with human existence; it must come into being—and not by necessity but in freedom. It is precisely for this reason that nonbeing is a continual possibility.

"Innocence is ignorance," Kierkegaard maintains. "In his innocence man is not determined as spirit but is soulishly determined in immediate unity with his natural condition. Spirit is dreaming in man" (*CoD*, 37). In the state of innocence man's existence is completely determined by his natural desires. Thus the innocence of which Kierkegaard speaks is not a state of being without desire. Kierkegaard agrees with the classical position of St. Augustine, that man is born with concupiscence. With his insistence upon "infantile sexuality" Freud also rejects the idealistic notion of a primal innocence in which there is the absence of desire. He would agree with Kierkegaard that man is born with concupiscence but that desire is ignorant of what it desires.

The ignorance of innocence is also an ignorance of good and evil, Kierkegaard asserts. To posit the existence of the ethical categories prior to the fall is to make the fall incomprehensible. Freud also rejects the notion of an innate knowledge of good and evil. But he locates the source of the ethical norm in society, whereas Kierkegaard gives it an ontological basis, as we shall see. In any event, both Kierkegaard and Freud agree that the ethical categories do not arise until after the fall, or

rather they are posited in the fall. In the state of innocence
man is not yet a self, but the category of guilt does not apply.
Until Spirit is posited there can be no guilt, for there is no
guilt without freedom.

But somehow the potential which is man is never fully realized, the relation which constitutes selfhood is always in disrelation, the ego finds itself divided against itself. Now this *is*
the nonbeing of guilt. Here the being which was possible has
been lost, and that which was man's most sublime potential
becomes the source of his greatest misery. What brings about
the transition from innocence to guilt? What can account for
the fall from potential being to actual nonbeing?

The Origin of the Sickness

Initially, as we have seen, Freud sought a purely somatic explanation for the sickness of the self. He first concluded that
the various neurotic symptoms result from frustrated libidinal
expression. He theorized that premature sexual stimulation
produces libidinal impulses which have no adequate physiological means of expression. Later, after puberty, this frustrated Libido finds expression in various neurotic symptoms.
In anxiety neurosis it is retained in a state of suspension which
may later find expression in phobias of various kinds; in the
case of hysterical neurosis the Libido is invested in some physical symptom; and in obsessional neurosis it is invested in substitutive ideas. In every case these libidinal expressions prove
to be inappropriate and ineffective modes and hence are considered to be neurotic.

Eventually however, Freud came to see that the libidinal
frustration is not the cause of anxiety but the effect. Libidinal
inhibition is a psychic defense against anxiety. Thus Freud
came to the same conclusion that Kierkegaard had reached by
another route—anxiety is the presupposition of neurosis. Or, as
Kierkegaard expressed it, dread is the presupposition of sin.
The problem of anxiety, therefore, became central to Freud's

theory of neurosis. What is the meaning of anxiety? What is its origin? What is its effect?

Freud locates the genesis of the anxiety response in the birth trauma. In the prenatal period the infant is utterly secure. His every need is immediately supplied. Indeed, he knows no need. But the event of birth puts an end to this blissful state. He is immediately thrust into the insecurity of existence in the world. In this experience the pattern of response to danger is established; all subsequent anxiety is a repetition of this fundamental response-pattern. Anxiety is an anticipation of impending danger, of an impending threat to the individual's security. It is a fear in advance of the danger, a dread "lest" something happen, an *"Angst* vor *etwas"* as Freud notes. After the birth event, the child's security is intimately related to his social situation, preeminently his family situation. Any threat to this social security is experienced as anxiety.

Now the infant's immediate impulsive mode of existence is a state of innocence. But in his innocence the individual encounters a social taboo. He soon discovers that certain impulsive behavior is prohibited by the social community in which he exists. His natural impulses therefore jeopardize his security, and there results the same psychological response-pattern which was established at birth, namely, anxiety. The initial response is a dread of authority, a response to the external prohibition. But when the prohibition has been internalized it becomes a dread of the superego, a dread of condemnation. Anxiety is thus an ambiguous thing. On the one hand there is the dread of the id which threatens to destroy the individual's social security, and on the other hand there is the dread of the superego with its condemnation. The self is thereby torn by conflict, at war with itself.

The similarity to Kierkegaard's understanding of the human situation in which the fall occurs is apparent. Kierkegaard also locates the origin of the sickness unto death in the anxiety inherent in the human situation. He does not seek an organic basis for anxiety, as Freud does, but his understanding of anxiety is no less ontological. Anxiety is a concomitant of human existence. There is no escape from dread. In the state of innocence there is no apparent dread, for Spirit or freedom has not yet been posited. However, dread is present but waiting, Kierkegaard says. Into the primal state of innocence there comes the word of prohibition. What is prohibited he does not say. Nor does he specify the social origin of the prohibition as Freud does. These problems are of secondary interest to Kierkegaard. He is concerned with its ontological significance. The explicit content of the prohibition is not important. What is important is the fact that man inevitably encounters a prohibiting word, a limiting factor, that which circumscribes his existence.

Like Freud, Kierkegaard perceives that man's response to the prohibition is dread or anxiety. But Kierkegaard sees deeper into the significance of the anxiety response. For Freud the anxiety is a dread of rejection by the social group in which man's security is grounded, and at the same time it is a dread of the id-impulses which jeopardize that social security. For Kierkegaard there is a deeper dimension to this dread. The prohibition reveals to man the possibility of a new mode of being, the peculiarly human mode of being—existence in freedom. In the state of innocence the individual is completely determined by his natural impulses, but the prohibition reveals to him the possibility of freedom. It may well be that the prohibition is directed at the instinctual drives, but what it reveals to him is that he possesses an innate capacity for self-determination, that he is responsible for his existence.

The "word of prohibition," Kierkegaard says, is immediately followed by the "word of judgment," the threat of the terrible. The individual is both fascinated and terrified by the possibility of existence in freedom. He finds himself in the ambiguous situation of dread. He desires what he dreads and he dreads what he desires. The basic anxiety, therefore, is not the dread of the Libido with its accompanying dread of social rejection. Social anxiety is simply a manifestation of the more

basic anxiety. Behind the social anxiety lies the dread of freedom with its consequent dread of judgment or condemnation.

Freud shows that the "word of prohibition" and the "word
of judgment" originate from the social context of human existence. The prohibition is experienced in the individual's
encounter with society. Kierkegaard does not specify the prohibition's social origin, but he does acknowledge that it is a
word spoken to the individual from without. "The voice of
prohibition and the punishment come from without" (*CoD*,
41). However, in a deeper sense, he maintains that the prohibition is voiced by the individual himself. The dialogue is an
inner dialogue. Freud, too, recognizes the internal dimension
of the word of prohibition. External frustration of the instinctual drives is not pathogenic, he notes; it is only when the
prohibition has been internalized that neurosis may result. The
initial anxiety may be a dread of the external prohibition, but
when the prohibition is internalized the dread becomes a dread
of inner condemnation.

Freud suggests that there are three possible responses to the
threatening situation. The initial impulse is *flight*, but flight
from an internal threat is impossible. The alternative is to
reject that which jeopardizes the individual's social security.
Instinct renunciation through *repression* is therefore the immediate response to the anxiety-producing situation. But repression is ultimately an inadequate expedient. To maintain
the repression requires a stronger defense. This is accomplished
by means of the development of the more or less permanent
defenses of the superego structures. Here the rejection is based
upon an internal *condemnation.* So it is that Freud can say,
"Repression is a preliminary phase of condemnation, something between flight and condemnation" (*CP*, IV, 84).

Kierkegaard's interpretation of the fall is not opposed to
Freud's; it simply explores a different dimension of the problem. As we have already seen, behind the dread of the libidinal
drives there lies a deeper dread, the dread of existence in freedom. Consequently, the deeper significance of repression is

that through it freedom is lost. The repression of the libidinal drives is essentially a flight from freedom. Instead of responsibly relating himself to the instinctual drives of the immediate self and employing them in the service of a transcendent norm, the individual denies, rejects, and represses the instinctual drives. What has been denied, however, is not just the libidinal desires, but also freedom and selfhood.

Empirically Freud observes that it is only now that the phenomenon of guilt arises. Earlier I rejected the notion that man possesses an innate moral sense; the phenomenon of guilt arises only after the prohibition has been internalized. The initial response of the individual to the social taboo was an immediate instinct renunciation. But this is not motivated solely by a dread of authority. Only after that authority has been internalized in the threat of condemnation posed by the superego can we observe a genuine sense of guilt. Freud notes that this sense of guilt is not necessarily related to an objective act. It is present in advance of the act. "The ego which knows on the one hand that it is innocent has on the other to experience a feeling of guilt and to carry a feeling of responsibility which it is unable to account for" (*PoA*, 51). Freud attributes this sense of guilt to the tension which exists between the libidinal impulse of the id and the internalized ideal of the ego.

The same ambiguous guilt is observed by Kierkegaard who, like Freud, rejects the notion that there exists in the state of innocence a knowledge of good and evil. The fall occurs in ignorance, and a knowledge of good and evil is not even posited until the fall. In the state of innocence man is potentially free, but he rejects freedom. For this he is guilty. But his guilt is ambiguous, Kierkegaard maintains. Man is guilty for it was by his own responsible flight that freedom and selfhood were lost. And yet it was in the grip of dread that the flight took place. But the dread was his dread, and the flight his flight. Guilt, it might be said, is the consequence of the persistence of Spirit in spite of its denial. Guilt is the tension between Spirit and the dread out of which the flight is continually motivated.

So once again it is apparent that Kierkegaard has plumbed a deeper dimension of the problem of guilt. Guilt may well be the tension between the instinctual drives and the superego, but this points to a more fundamental guilt. Behind the social guilt there lies an ontological guilt. Social guilt is a reminder that one is essentially free but has lost his freedom. In the persistence of the libidinal drives, the possibility of freedom is persistently present, and in its renunciation freedom is also renounced. In the act of repression the individual has employed his freedom to deny his freedom.

In summary, though the two interpretations of the aetiology of the sickness of the self seem to be quite disparate, the essential elements are the same. In each there is a primal state of innocence in which the individual's behavior is determined by his natural desires and in which there is no knowledge of good and evil. In both interpretations the potential to selfhood is present in this primal state. In both, the immediate "self" encounters a taboo or prohibition which makes this potentiality a possibility. The possibility of selfhood is not realized because of an intermediate state of dread or anxiety which the prohibition evokes. In each interpretation selfhood is vitiated in a flight which is motivated by the state of dread. And, in both, the consequence is guilt.

Each man has interpreted the basic elements in the fall from potential being to actual nonbeing in the light of his own central category. Freud's interpretation is basically a somatic reduction valid on one level of analysis. But Kierkegaard insists that human existence includes a third dimension in addition to the somatic and the psychic, namely, the pneumatic or spiritual; and it is this dimension which he seeks to explore. The essence of selfhood is not just Libido, but Spirit. The anxiety is not just a dread of libidinal existence, but a dread of existence in freedom. And what is renounced by the flight is not just the instinctual libidinal drive, but Spirit, and hence, selfhood.

The Potentiation of the Sickness

Both Kierkegaard and Freud posit a kind of gradient in the sickness of the self. There are varying degrees of nonbeing. The loss of selfhood is progressive. Kierkegaard noted this in his classification of the types of despair. First there is "unconscious despair"—despair which is unaware that it is despair. The self has lost its selfhood but is not even conscious of the loss. This is a subtle type of despair, precisely because it is the form of the sickness which infects us all. The self has capitulated to the consensus of the crowd. It conforms to social expectation. It no longer exercises its selfhood, though it continues to live with the illusion that it is a self. Freud does not explicitly deal with this form of despair, though an implicit criticism of the cultural norm pervades his writing.

I have concentrated on the more extreme forms of the sickness, what Kierkegaard termed "conscious despair." He distinguishes two varieties of conscious despair: the "despair of weakness" and the "despair of defiance." The former deals with the phenomena which Freud calls the "transference neuroses," while the latter corresponds to "psychosis." In the former there is a kind of capitulation to the demands of the superego with varying degrees of loss of selfhood, while in the latter there is a defiant rejection of the superego and the social reality it represents. Freud's careful clinical research into these two forms of despair constitutes a significant confirmation of Kierkegaard's intuitive analysis. This can be seen in their respective treatments of the object of dread in the two forms of the sickness.

Kierkegaard notes that in the primal state of innocence dread is without an object. It is a dread of a possibility vaguely perceived, the dread of a possible mode of being—namely, existence in freedom. But in the flight from freedom, the nothing becomes a something. With the fall, good and evil are posited. The infinite, the possible, the eternal become identified with the good; while the finite, the necessary, the temporal become synonymous with the evil. Thus the objectless dread receives an object. The dread of nothing becomes a dread of something. Two forms of dread are now present: dread of the evil, and dread of the good. The former corresponds to the despair of weakness; the latter, to the despair of defiance.

Freud makes a similar analysis, expressed of course in his characteristic categories. He is also aware of the fundamental objectless nature of anxiety. Indeed it is this characteristic which distinguishes anxiety from fear. Anxiety has no objective referent, while fear has. In fact, the neurotic defenses can be understood in part as an attempt to convert anxiety into fear, to give anxiety an object. The primal anxiety of birth is objectless. Its subsequent recurrence is also without an object. It is a dread of something which is not yet, a dread in anticipation of a possibility. In its purest form, Freud refers to it as a free-floating anxiety. But with the fall, i.e. subsequent to repression, anxiety receives an object. Good and evil are now posited. Good is identified with the demands of the superego, and evil with the desires of the id. Thus dread may take either of two forms. It may become a dread of the id, the "evil," wherein the ego accedes to the demands of the superego and represses the id, in which case neurosis results. Or it may become a dread of the superego, the "good," wherein the ego aligns itself with the id and renounces the social reality in which it has its existence, in which case psychosis results.

Normally the individual remains "in the good," as Kierkegaard puts it, and lives "in dread of the evil." He dreads succumbing to the finite, the necessary, and the temporal. His identity is defined in terms of the good, i.e. the infinite, the possible, and the eternal. To succumb to the evil is to lose his very identity. Hence, he dreads the evil. The appropriate response to the threat of the evil is a synthesis of the finite and the infinite. Translated into Freudian terminology this means that the normal individual derives his identity from the social norms as incorporated in the superego. This constitutes his "good." He dreads the threat of the Libido, for to succumb to its demands is to lose his identity. But he cannot deny the libidinal drive altogether. Consequently, he sublimates it into modes of expression which are acceptable to the superego. Libido is transmuted into Eros as it is subordinated to the life-instinct.

To be sure, this is a form of despair. It is the incipient form which Kierkegaard calls "unconscious despair." It is universal, as both Kierkegaard and Freud acknowledge. For Kierkegaard it has the universality of sin. For Freud it is the collective neurosis which saves the individual from a personal neurosis. But in the more pernicious form of despair there is no such creative response on the part of the self. Here the individual's response is repression, not sublimation. The Libido becomes subject to the death-instinct instead of the life-instinct. Freedom is lost. The individual is in bondage to the evil. He is bound to the libidinal drive just as surely as he would be had he succumbed to it. But it is an ironic bondage. He is bound by negation. Most of his energy is expended in negating the Libido rather than using it in the service of the good. This is the "despair of weakness." The individual yearns for freedom, but he has not the strength to break the pattern.

His attempts to recover his selfhood take the form of remorse. He never breaks with the bondage which is the consequence of his dread of the evil, and yet he regrets this bondage. He is tied to the evil through guilt, but he cannot escape the guilt. He is simply continually remorseful. Freud also recognizes the futility of remorse in freeing oneself of neurotic guilt. This is seen most clearly in his treatment of obsessional neurosis. Here the guilt is clearly present in the efforts to undo the "wrong" through various acts of atonement. But the obsessive compulsion of remorse can never accomplish what it intends. It can never remove the guilt. Freud describes the response of remorse as an "endless epilogue."

The same is true of the other two forms of neurosis where the ego's response to guilt is punishment and isolation. The self-inflicted punishments of hysterical neurosis are as ineffectual as the compulsive atonements of obsessional neurosis, for here the relationship to reality is even more attenuated. And the solitary confinement of anxiety neurosis verges on a complete break with reality. But the prognosis of this kind of despair is not hopeless, for the individual is still "in the good," to use Kierkegaard's term. The ego sustains a relation to reality, however tenuous. And so long as this is the case, there is hope.

There is an even more pernicious form of dread, however, which Kierkegaard discerned. It is the "dread of the good," a dread which refuses to be helped. Kierkegaard is surprisingly contemporary in his perception of the "epinosic gain" of the sickness of the self which legislates against therapy. When illness becomes a way of life, when the benefits of sickness exceed the pain it causes, the individual refuses to be helped. He says, as Kierkegaard so graphically put it, "Let me be the miserable man I am." He stands in dread of possible relief. He prefers to exist in guilt. Freud also notes this repeatedly in his therapeutic work. He says, for example, "There is something in these people that sets itself against their recovery and dreads its approach as though it were a danger" (*E&I*, 70-71). There is a kind of moral factor, a sense of guilt which apparently finds atonement in the illness. This is what Kierkegaard calls the "demoniacal."

Again Kierkegaard employs the concept of Spirit or freedom as the interpretive principle. Dread of the good—the demoniacal—is a spiritual phenomenon. Though the dread of the evil is the consequence of a flight from freedom, the individual still remains essentially free inasmuch as he lives in dread of unfreedom. He is yet in the good, for he exists in dread of the evil. In the demoniacal, however, it is freedom itself which the individual dreads and continually renounces. The continuity of his self is inextricably tied up with the state of unfreedom. To lose this bondage is to lose his "self," so to speak. The unfreedom is apparent in the "close reserve or "shut-upness" or "introversion" of the self, as the Danish term *Indesluttedhed* is variously translated. The individual is closed within himself; he has shut himself off from reality. He is no longer related to a transcendent reality and hence his existence is empty of meaning, "vacuous," as Kierkegaard terms it. He is also unfree with respect to time. Out of his shut-upness there breaks forth unfreely the terrible monologue which is just as quickly gone. This phenomenon Kierkegaard refers to as "the sudden," suggesting the autonomy of the sickness over which the self has lost control.

Still freedom cannot be completely obliterated. It is present even in this unfreedom. It reveals its presence in the renewed terror and flight of the demoniac when he is offered the possibility of freedom. It reveals itself against the will of the demoniac in the "ventriloquism" of his behavior which surreptitiously says what he cannot openly reveal. Man is a relation between body and soul—a relation sustained in freedom. But, "so soon as the subordinate relationship comes to an end, so soon as the body revolts, so soon as freedom enters into conspiracy with it against itself, there unfreedom is present as the demoniacal" (*CoD*, 121). This is freedom lost somaticpsychically.

This is what Freud is talking about when he says that psychosis occurs when the ego aligns itself with the id against reality. As we have seen, Freud conceived of the superego as the structure by means of which the self relates itself to its social reality. The superego is an internally appropriated ideal or norm. Selfhood requires the development of this structure, but neurosis and psychosis are the perversions of it. When the ego falls into bondage to this ego ideal and is dominated by it, it exists in guilt. It has fallen into the sickness of the self. The form which this sickness takes depends upon the type of defense which the ego chooses. If it aligns itself with the superego to repress the id drives in the attempt to relieve the guilt, neurosis results. But if the ego aligns itself with the id against reality, psychosis is the consequence. So intense is the guilt that instead of sublimating the Libido into creative modes of social expression, or repressing the Libido in a neurotic effort to avoid guilt, the ego gives up its painful relation to reality entirely. It aligns itself with the id, and seeks to remodel reality in accordance with the demands of the id.

Freud's best analysis of this phenomenon is found in his treatment of melancholia, which corresponds in every respect to Kierkegaard's description of the demoniacal. In melancholia there is a "pure culture of the death-instinct" (*E&I*, 77). It is truly a sickness unto death. "In fact it often enough succeeds in driving the ego into death, if the latter does not protect itself from the tyrant in time by a revulsion into mania" (*E&I*, 77). Freud gives a typically libidinal interpretation of this sickness. He says that instead of transferring the Libido to another object, as in the transference neuroses, the Libido is withdrawn into the ego. The ego becomes its own object. This is what Kierkegaard refers to as "the negating retrenchment of the ego" (*CoD*, 115). The result is the same ambivalence toward the self which the self formerly had toward its external object. That is, the self now directs toward itself not only the love but also the hostility which was formerly directed toward the external object. The depressive phase of melancholia is the consequence of the latter, while the manic phase indicates a temporary dominance of the narcissistic love.

The similarity between these two interpretations of nonbeing is striking in spite of their radically different orientations. Both acknowledge the psychosomatic nature of the sickness of the self. In neurosis, or sin, the psychic element (the superego) dominates the relationship and the somatic element is repressed. In psychosis, or the demoniacal, the somatic element (the id) dominates and the psychic element is rejected. But this is as far as Freud's analysis takes him. Kierkegaard, on the other hand, insists that there is also a pneumatic dimension to the sickness of the self. If the self is a synthesis of body and soul, a synthesis which is sustained by Spirit, then in the loss of either the first element or the second there is also the loss of the third. In psychosis, when the id dominates the relationship and the superego is rejected, the relationship to the transcendent reality is lost and with it selfhood. But the relationship to the transcendent is also lost when the superego dominates the relationship and the id is rejected, for here the transcendent is identified with the social ideal. Here the relation to the eternal is lost just as surely as when the self renounces the eternal.

The self to be a self must continually appropriate the eternal in time. It must give existential enactment to the eternal. It must constantly finitize the infinite, without identifying it with the particular form in which it has been appropriated. In short, as we have seen before, true selfhood requires the maintenance of an absolute relation to the Absolute *alone,* and a relative relation to the relative.

The Cultural Factor in the Sickness

When I dealt with the prohibition or taboo which evokes the anxiety that precipitates the flight from selfhood, I noted the cultural factor in the sickness of the self. But the importance which both Kierkegaard and Freud place on this element in terms of the object of dread and mode of flight warrants further consideration.

Freud gave increasing emphasis to the cultural factor in the aetiology of neurosis. It is culture which imposes limitations upon the individual's freedom; culture enunciates the prohibition. This prohibition is the incitement to both selfhood and neurosis. In response to it the self comes into existence. It is culture which provides the content of the superego. But it is also in response to this cultural taboo that the neurotic defenses are erected. Thus, guilt is for Freud a cultural phenomenon.

Kierkegaard, on the other hand, does not make culture the locus of the prohibition and hence of guilt. The prohibition is more basic than culture; it is inherent in the fundamental ontology of human existence. The prohibition represents the essential limit of human existence, the limit of selfhood. It signifies the finitude, the necessity, the temporality of human existence, and this is not dependent upon culture. It is not a function of culture; it is prior to culture.

But, while Kierkegaard does not locate the prohibition in culture, he does recognize the important role which culture plays in the sickness of the self. The cultural nexus in which man finds himself contributes an additional factor to the prohibition, a "more" Kierkegaard terms it. The flight from freedom cannot be attributed to culture, in spite of the increasingly significant role which culture plays in predisposing the individual toward the loss of selfhood. However great an influence the cultural context may exert upon the individual, the flight is still *his* flight. It still takes place in freedom. But it is true that the cultural nexus may quantitatively contribute to the prohibition, and hence increase the dread out of which the fall proceeds.

Kierkegaard cites the way in which Western culture has come to identify the self, the sensual, and the temporal with sin and to make these the locus of the prohibition. But none of these are in themselves sinful, he insists. They are essential elements in human existence. It is only when the dialectic between the temporal and the eternal is vitiated that these aspects of human being become symptomatic of sin. But the culture into which the individual is born has come to identify these elements with sin. It makes them taboo, and so heightens the dread which the individual experiences. Thus, when Freud suggests that it is culture which posits the prohibition and that this prohibition is essentially a sexual taboo, he is not wrong. But there is a deeper dimension to this phenomenon which Kierkegaard perceives. He would maintain that the prohibition is the existential limit posed by man's finitude, necessity, and temporality. Culture gives this limit an objective form—cultural taboo. Thus the existential prohibition is augmented by culture.

Furthermore, Kierkegaard notes a difference between cul-

tures with respect to the object of dread. The aesthetic culture
has sought to escape the dread of freedom by positing fate as
the ultimate reality. By getting rid of freedom and supposing
that human existence is fatalistically determined, it hopes to
be rid of dread. But Kierkegaard perceptively observes the
presence of freedom in the dread of fate. In the consultation
of the oracle freedom is manifested; and in the ambiguity of
the oracle dread remains. Dread, then, persists in the form of
that which was posited to escape dread. Freud also observed
the ambiguity involved in the Greek solution to the problem
of dread. The Greeks posited the gods to account for the
exigencies of human existence, hoping thereby to enable the
individual to control his destiny by influencing the gods. But
the gods themselves were subject to a higher fate. Freud, with
Kierkegaard, rejects this cultural response as infantile, a neurotic defense against the dread of freedom.

Ethical cultures, in their effort to escape from dread, posit
law or an ethical absolute as the ultimate reality. It is thought
that in the perfect fulfillment of the law there would be no
anxiety. But again, as Kierkegaard observes, dread persists in
the form of guilt. The focus of the anxiety has shifted from
the aesthetic to the ethical—from the somatic form of dread
toward the spiritual—but dread is no less present. Again, Freud
has amplified the point. As we have seen, he was deeply critical of Western culture. To him it is a culture built on guilt. The
instinct renunciation which it requires is self-defeating. Renunciation of the libidinal drives produces hostility toward
culture, the source of the prohibition. This, in turn, requires
additional strictures against the hostility which threatens to
destroy the culture. This hostility which therefore cannot be
expressed in society is turned inward upon the self in the form
of guilt. Through the superego the self is aware of even un-
expressed desires and feelings. Consequently, guilt is experienced even where there is no objective culpability. In addition,
the taboos which were posited to avoid anxiety result in a
heightening of the id-impulses, which in turn requires addition-

al social restraints. Thus is created an ever increasing burden of instinctual renunciation and guilt. While both Kierkegaard and Freud refer to the Jewish culture as a case in point, the Puritanical culture of colonial America and the Victorian culture of Freud's own time are also illustrative.

Finally, in a spiritual or religious culture, in Kierkegaard's sense of the term, freedom is affirmed as the ultimate reality in spite of the dread which is its concomitant. Here the true locus of dread is recognized. That which is actually dreaded in aesthetic fate or ethical guilt is freedom itself, or Spirit. But dreadful as freedom is, there is one thing to be dreaded more —spiritlessness. Dread, rightly conceived, is a dread of unfreedom or sin. Insofar as popular religion is the continuation of pagan religion in Christian garb, Freud is right in rejecting it as an infantile projection of the Oedipus complex. It is simply a new fatalism. And insofar as modern religion is simply an extension of the guilt complex of an ethical culture, Freud is right in denouncing it as collective obsessional neurosis. What Freud calls for is a secular version of Kierkegaard's "religious existence." He envisions a culture founded on reason within the limits of necessity. This is not unlike Kierkegaard's concept of religious existence which is a synthesis of possibility and necessity. In Freud's stubborn confidence in reason, within the limits of necessity, we have a rationalistic version of Kierkegaard's faith to exist in freedom, within the limits of necessity.

Part Three
The Restoration of
Selfhood

7. Kierkegaard's Concept of the Christian Therapeutic

The Problem of Selfhood

The Concept of Recollection

When Kierkegaard addressed himself to the problem of the restoration of selfhood he found it very difficult to get beyond Socrates. Indeed, preferring Socratic ignorance to Christian pretension, he chided the speculative theologians of his time for their presumptuous claim to have gone beyond Socrates. "To have made an advance upon Socrates without even having understood what he understood, is at any rate not 'Socratic'" (*CUP,* 183). This error I do not intend to make. Consequently, I will begin my investigation of the restoration of selfhood with Socrates's statement of the problem and his doctrine of *recollection,* before proceeding to Kierkegaard's understanding of the problem and his *repetition* doctrine.

The question at hand is that of truth, "the eternal and essential truth, the truth which has an essential relationship to an existing individual because it pertains essentially to existence" (*CUP,* 83), as Kierkegaard puts it. Human existence is historical. The self must become what it is. Hence, man is a being in quest of the truth of his existence. But the task of ascertaining this truth—the truth man is to become—is profoundly problematic. Socrates saw clearly man's paradoxical situation with respect to truth: One cannot seek for what he knows, since he already knows it; but neither can he seek for what he does not know, since he would not even know for what to seek.[1] Or to put it another way: It is the task of man to become a self, but he cannot make a start at this without presupposing what it is that constitutes selfhood, and that is precisely what he does not know.

Socrates's resolution of the paradox is given in his doctrine of recollection. This doctrine asserts that truth or virtue is immanent in man, a "knowledge" which he has "forgotten," so to speak. Consequently, all learning is a kind of remembering, a recollection, *anamnesis*. The therapeutic problem, therefore, is to evoke from the obscure reaches of man's memory the truth which he already possesses. Hence the Socratic dictum, "Know thyself," becomes the therapeutic key.

Now when Kierkegaard says that to make an advance upon Socrates we must at least understand what he understood, he means that any answer which claims to go beyond Socrates must take as seriously as he did the paradoxical character of the human situation. There is, however, implicit in Socrates's doctrine of recollection a presupposition which paves the way for a theoretical circumvention of the existential predicament. His doctrine presupposes that there is inherent in man an eternal essence which, at least in principle, one may come to know through recollection. This presupposition invites all kinds of abstract speculation concerning the eternal truth of man. Existentially this is utterly intolerable since it postpones selfhood until one has ascertained the ideal. Beginning with the "what" it never gets to the "how," because, as Socrates understood so well, objectively the individual always remains in a paradoxical relation to the truth.

But, as Kierkegaard observes, Socrates was always departing from his doctrine of recollection in order to exist. Socrates's theoretical answer to the human predicament was always being nullified by his existential answer. Kierkegaard sums up the significance of the doctrine of recollection for Socrates as "the constantly rejected possibility of engaging in speculation"

1. See the *Meno*.

(*CUP*, 184). His passionate concern with existence protected Socrates from pursuing the implications of his doctrine.

Thus there are two fundamentally opposite ways of approaching the question of the truth of man's existence. One may approach the problem objectively or subjectively, but he cannot do both simultaneously. If he approaches the question objectively, subjectivity is lost. In becoming objective the subject loses that which constitutes its essence, i.e. subjectivity. Conversely, if the question is approached subjectively, objectivity is lost; truth becomes objectively uncertain. The former method seeks to know the truth at the cost of being; the latter seeks to be the truth at the cost of knowing. In Kierkegaard's own words:

> When the question of truth is raised in an objective manner, reflection is directed objectively to the truth, as an object to which the knower is related. Reflection is not focused upon the relationship, however, but upon the question of whether it is the truth to which the knower is related. If only the object to which he is related is the truth, the subject is accounted to be in the truth. When the question of the truth is raised subjectively, reflection is directed subjectively to the nature of the individual's relationship; if only the mode of this relationship is in the truth, the individual is in the truth even if he should happen to be thus related to what is not true. [*CUP*, 178]

The question is, which method shall we employ in the search for selfhood? Kierkegaard suggests that the answer is self-evident to any *existing* individual, i.e. to any one who is concerned with existing. The existing man is inescapably confronted with the problem of becoming. But who is he to become? The individual who chooses to pursue the objective way enters into a lengthy parenthesis, an extended approximation process, during which he must indefinitely postpone existing. He who chooses the way of subjectivity is immediately thrust into becoming, even if that which he has chosen to become is ultimately false. To be a self is to be a subject; hence, the highest truth for human being is subjectivity. Thus we arrive at Kierkegaard's definition of truth: "An objective uncertainty held fast in an appropriation-process of the most passionate inwardness is the truth, the highest truth attainable for an *existing* individual" (*CUP*, 182). It is precisely this objective uncertainty which incites the infinite passion of subjectivity by virtue of which one's selfhood is affirmed. Thus, Socrates's existential refusal to escape from existence by means of his doctrine of recollection is his wisdom. It is for this reason that Kierkegaard can say, "Socrates was in the truth by virtue of his ignorance" (*CUP*, 183).

The Concept of Repetition

Socrates was limited in his understanding of man's dilemma, however. The Socratic perception of the paradoxical predicament of man may indeed force us to acknowledge that subjectivity is truth, but paradoxically we then discover that we cannot be subjective. The paradox is paradoxical in itself. Subjectivity is truth, but only if it "begins by positing the opposite principle: That subjectivity is untruth" (*CUP*, 185). That is to say, that "subjectivity in beginning upon the task of becoming the truth through a subjectifying process, is in the difficulty that it is already untruth" (*CUP*, 185). The subject has already surrendered his subjectivity. As was indicated earlier, the first act of the self is to renounce subjectivity. This is the original sin. The individual is no longer a self because he will not be a self. His problem is therefore not ignorance but sin. Christianity knows that this is the crux of the problem. We remain in untruth, not because we do not *know* what selfhood is, but because we will not *risk* subjectivity. Existence has us doubly in its bondage: first, on the level of which Socrates was aware, the epistemological paradox; and second, on the level of which Christianity is aware, the existential paradox.

The problem of selfhood thus becomes more a problem of *repetition* than of *recollection*. What is needed is not so much an occasion for recollecting a forgotten essence, as an occasion for repeating a lost existence. So long as it is thought possible to recover selfhood through recollection, one is protected from the profound inwardness of subjectivity. But, Kierkegaard notes:

> The more difficult it is made for him to take himself out of existence by way of recollection, the more profound is the inwardness that his existence may have in existence; and when it is made impossible for him, when he is held so fast in existence that the back door of recollection is forever closed to him, then his inwardness will be the most profound possible. [*CUP*, 186-87]

It then becomes necessary to enter eternity "forwards," as Kierkegaard says, since it is no longer possible to relate to it "backwards." Socrates understood the dubiety of taking oneself out of existence and back into the eternal through speculation; Christianity knows it to be impossible.

The contrast between the Greek quest for selfhood by way of recollection and the Christian way of repetition is clarified in Kierkegaard's discussion of the Greek and Christian understanding of time and eternity in *The Concept of Dread* (pp. 76ff.). For the Greek, the eternal lies in the past to which one relates himself by recollection. It has no essential relation to the present moment. Time is simply a "going-by," and the present moment is merely that infinitesimal point which divides the future from the past. For the Christian, the eternal is always the future to which the individual continually relates his present, and which thereby determines his present. The present moment, therefore, has radical significance as the point where time and eternity meet. Kierkegaard summarizes the Greek view as follows: "The Greek eternity lies behind, as the past into which one enters only backwards" (*CoD*, 78), i.e. by recollection. He could have added: The Christian eternity lies ahead, as the future into which one enters only forwards, i.e. by repetition. In place of the determinism of the past, Christianity offers a determinism of the future. The former is bondage, the latter is freedom.

Kierkegaard pursued the question of the recovery of freedom in a little essay entitled "Repetition." He wrote:

> Repetition and recollection are the same movement, only in opposite directions; for what is recollected has been, is repeated backwards, whereas repetition properly so called is recollected forwards. Therefore repetition, if it is possible, makes a man happy, whereas recollection makes him unhappy. [*Rep*, 3-4]

Recollection is a backward-oriented repetition of life. Repetition is a forward-oriented recollection, a recollection of existence in continual relation to the future. The two are, therefore, the same movement. Only the orientation is different. But therein lies the difference between the despair of bondage and the joy of freedom.

Recollection reminds us that we are the product of our past, that we can understand who we are by recalling who we have been. But repetition affirms that our present self is also determined by the future, that our existence is yet open. Without both categories, recollection and repetition, life is without meaning, for the former provides the substance or necessity of our existence and the latter provides possibility.

> Men are divided into two great classes: Those who predominantly live in hope, and those who predominantly live in recollection. Both have a wrong relation to time. The healthy individual lives at once both in hope and in recollection, and only thereby does his life acquire true and substantial continuity. So, then, he has hope and does not wish, like those who live off recollection, to return backward in time. [*E/O*, II, 144-45]

Thus selfhood is a mode of being which sustains both the backward orientation of recollection and the forward orientation of hope in the dialectical relation which is repetition.

Kierkegaard concludes, "He who would only hope is cowardly, he who would only recollect is a voluptuary, but he who wills repetition is a man" (*Rep*, 5).

The Restoration of Selfhood

The Problem of Communication

To be sure, the problem of selfhood was intensely personal for Kierkegaard, but he was also concerned with the question of how the existential truth can be communicated to others. He was convinced that the nature of the truth to be communicated has a great deal to do with the method to be employed in its communication. If what one desires to communicate is a body of objective data, then some form of objective communication is appropriate. However, if what one desires to communicate is not objective but subjective, if what is to be communicated is in fact a mode of being, surely the objective method is both inappropriate and ineffectual.

> Suppose that someone wished to communicate the following conviction: Truth is inwardness; there is no objective truth, but the truth consists in personal appropriation. Suppose him to display great zeal and enthusiasm for the propagation of this truth, since if people could only be made to listen to it they would of course be saved; suppose he announced it on all possible occasions, and succeeded in moving not only those who perspire easily, but also the hard-boiled temperaments: what then? Why then, there would doubtless be found a few laborers, who had hitherto stood idle in the market-place, and only after hearing this call went to work in the vineyard—engaging themselves to proclaim this doctrine to all. And then what? Then he would have contradicted himself. [*CUP*, 71]

In fact, as Kierkegaard points out, there is here a double contradiction. First, this person's method contradicts his message; and, second, the results reveal the message was never really communicated. Since this fancied evangelist sought to communicate the truth of subjectivity objectively it is little wonder that he only succeeded in obtaining "town criers of inwardness," a contradiction in itself. What was intended to be communicated was a mode of being and what was actually communicated was a doctrine *about* a mode of being. This is not communication.

The reason for the failure does not reside in the degree of skill which the evangelist possessed but in the method employed. Subjectivity simply cannot be directly communicated, for its direct expression is precisely objectivity (*CUP*, 232). The essence of subjectivity is vitiated when it is given objective expression. Similarly, the reception of the subjective mode of being is not accomplished by the direct reflection of the objective content of the communication. This is merely an "echo," Kierkegaard declares. The authentic reproduction of subjectivity in the recipient has more of the character of a "resonance" in which the original proclamation is absent (*CUP*, 232).

Consequently, Kierkegaard sought to develop and perfect an "indirect method of communication"—taking his cue from Socrates, he called it a "maieutic method"—which would require the subject of the communication to be subjective and draw his own conclusions. Kierkegaard's early efforts in this regard were chiefly literary. He wrote under clever pseudonymns which revealed, as much as they concealed, his intent. In this literary production he tried to embody other modes of being in order to puncture their pretensions. His pen was an effective weapon filled with "thoughts which wound from behind."

In Kierkegaard's posthumously published "report to history," the point of this literary camouflage was made clear—to dispel the illusions under which men live. "There is an immense difference . . . [between] the case of a man who is ignorant and is to have a piece of knowledge imparted to him . . . and the case of a man who is under an illusion and must first be delivered from that" (*PoV*, 40). In the latter case direct communication is impossible. "Direct communication presupposes that the receiver's ability to receive is undisturbed. But here such is not the case; an illusion stands in the way" (*PoV*, 40). The first task is to remove the illusion, and this is accomplished by means of a deception. By "deception" Kierkegaard means that "one does not begin *directly* with the matter one wants to communicate, but begins by accepting the other man's illusion as good money" (*PoV*, 40). His literary production sought to do just that. He insinuated himself into the aesthetic mode of being, and sought to embody in his writings the very essence of that mode, in order better to evoke from his readers the discovery of the illusion under which they live.

Still, the literary indirect method of communication represents a premature expression of Kierkegaard's understanding of existential communication. He came to see that the efficacy of the indirect method of communication of Christianity was dependent upon the recipient's prior knowledge of it. Just as the Socratic maieutic is premised on an immanent truth which the method helps the learner recollect, so Kierkegaard's indirect method is premised on a prior knowledge of Christianity to which the individual can be recalled. But Kierkegaard, in contrast to Socrates, did not believe that the truth is inherent in man. Consequently, even the indirect method if communication is inadequate.

> The communication of Christianity must ultimately end in 'bearing witness', the maieutic form can never be final. For truth, from the Christian point of view, does not lie in the subject (as Socrates understood it) but in a revelation which must be proclaimed. In Christendom the maieutic form can certainly be used, simply because the majority in fact live under the impression that they are Christians. But since Christianity is Christianity the maieuticer must become the witness . . . though different

from the direct witness in that he has been through the
process of becoming one. [*Jour,* 809]

Thus, in the end the communication of subjectivity or selfhood depends upon its existential enactment in a witness.

Kierkegaard is careful to distinguish this existential communication from the direct communication he has so consistently rejected. The shift does not represent a shift from
subjective communication to objective communication, but a
deepening comprehension of what constitutes subjective
communication. Kierkegaard is saying that pseudonymous
tricks will not suffice to communicate the truth of subjectivity. The efficacy of the indirect method is limited to dis-
pelling illusions. But, when the work of negation is accomplished, the positive witness can only be made by one who
"has been through the process of becoming one," that is, by
one who has himself become a self. The former work can be
performed pseudonymously; the latter, never.

The distinction between these two forms of indirect communication is sharpened in *Training in Christianity*. After
asserting the impossibility of the direct communication of selfhood, Kierkegaard declares:

> The opposite of direct communication is indirect commu-
> nication. The latter can be produced in either of two ways.
> Indirect communication can be produced by the art of
> reduplicating the communication . . . [or] by the relation-
> ship between the communication and the communicator.
> [*TiC,* 132-33]

The former "consists in reducing oneself, the communicator,
to nobody, something purely objective" (*TiC,* 132), but, if
genuine reduplication of selfhood is desired, then decisive significance must be attached to the existence of the communicator. "All communication which has regard to 'existence' requires a communicator—in other words, the communication is
the reduplication of that which is communicated; to redupli-

cate is to 'exist' in what one understands" (*TiC*, 133). Thus Kierkegaard concluded that selfhood is communicated by neither the preacher nor the confessor but by the witness who has himself become a self.

The Dynamics of Repetition

We have been considering Kierkegaard's therapeutic method, with its aim of the restoration of lost selfhood through repetition. Now the dynamics of repetition must be examined. The self has lost its selfhood in the attempt to find security in the finite, the necessary, the temporal. The essential thing, of course, is to restore the proper priority of ends, to establish an absolute relation to the absolute *telos* and a relative relation to the relative *teloi*. But what "movements of the spirit" are necessary to bring about the repetition of the selfhood which has been lost?

In *Fear and Trembling* Kierkegaard suggests that a double movement is necessary—a movement involving resignation and faith. Before an absolute relation to the absolute can be effected, the individual must relinquish his commitment to the relative ends which have become determinative of his existence. This does not result in a blissful amnesia. It is not a forgetfulness which would lightly dismiss the self one has become. Indeed, Kierkegaard notes, "it is a contradiction to forget the whole content of one's life and yet remain the same man" (*F&T*, 54). Resignation involves the recollection of the whole historical self one has become. But it is a recollection oriented toward the future. The remembrance is painful, for it involves the relinquishment of those finite ends which have come to be determinative of one's existence. But it is also joyful because it frees the self to become a self. It is, in truth, a dying to self to find oneself.

The dying to self is not yet the finding of selfhood, and resignation is not faith. Resignation is simply the prerequisite of faith. "Faith has resignation as its presupposition" (*F&T*, 58), Kierkegaard says. He elaborates:

> The infinite resignation is the last stage prior to faith, so
> that one who has not made this movement has not faith;
> for only in the infinite resignation do I become clear to
> myself with respect to my eternal validity, and only then
> can there be any question of grasping existence by virtue
> of faith. [*F&T,* 57]

In the act of resignation the eternal validity of the self is
affirmed. In the renunciation of those finite commitments
which are determinative of its action, the self demonstrates its
transcendence over the finite. But, while the eternal significance of the self is affirmed in the act of resignation, its temporal significance requires a second movement—faith.

Repetition requires the renunciation of the finite ends which
determine one's existence and usurp his selfhood. But, since
human existence is existence in the world, selfhood involves a
relation not only to the eternal but also to the temporal. There
must be a paradoxical movement back into the world. What is
required is the dialectic of existing in the context of finite
ends while renouncing their absolute claim. Or, to put it more
positively, it is the process of living in the temporal by virtue
of the eternal. But this requires a special kind of courage.

> A purely human courage is required to renounce the whole
> of the temporal to gain the eternal. . . . But a paradoxical
> and humble courage is required to grasp the whole of the
> temporal by virtue of the absurd, and this is the courage of
> faith. [*F&T,* 59]

In short, the first movement, resignation, requires a kind of
heroic courage, while the second movement, faith, requires a
humble courage akin to trust.

The Pathetic Factor

Not content with this brief exploration into the problem of
the restoration of selfhood, Kierkegaard continued to probe
the depths of the "existential pathos" involved. Resignation,

he discovered, was simply the initial expression of the existential pathos. Essentially the existential pathos is suffering; more specifically, its decisive expression is the consciousness of guilt. These ever deepening dimensions of the existential pathos are explored extensively in the last half of the *Concluding Unscientific Postscript,* which I will briefly summarize.

Resignation

The initial expression of the self's relation to its absolute *telos* is resignation. That is to say, the absolute relation to the absolute *telos* manifests itself initially in the renunciation of all relative *teloi.* Every other desire must be subordinated to the ultimate goal of selfhood—"eternal happiness," as Kierkegaard also expresses it. He says, "Now if for any individual an eternal happiness is his highest good, this will mean that all finite satisfactions are volitionally relegated to the status of what may have to be renounced in favor of an eternal happiness" (*CUP,* 350).

Such a passionate commitment to the absolute *telos* transforms the individual's existence. "Even a relative end transforms a man's existence partially" (*CUP,* 352), but the absolute *telos* transforms the individual's existence absolutely. An absolute relation to the absolute *telos* means there is nothing, no finite goal whatsoever, that the individual would not relinquish for the sake of his eternal happiness.

Such a *telos* is never exhausted in time. In the case of a relative end, a certain portion of time will need to be devoted to its realization, but the absolute *telos* requires the whole of time. Eternal happiness, or selfhood, is not a goal to be achieved—and then one can go on to something else. It is the nature of such a goal "that the whole of time and of existence should be the period of striving" (*CUP,* 356). Furthermore, this goal is never exhausted in relative ends. To be sure, the individual lives in the realm of relative ends. He cannot escape the relativities of worldly existence. He must continually act in the concrete medium of relative ends and means, but these do not exhaust the meaning of his life. "The individual is in truth in the relative ends with his direction toward the absolute *telos;* but he is not so in them as to exhaust himself in them" (*CUP*, 359). Kierkegaard is not denying the necessity of finite commitments to relative ends. "But," he says, "the relationship to the absolute *telos* cannot pour itself exhaustively into the relative ends, because the absolute relationship may require the renunciation of them all" (*CUP*, 363).

Now, when we talk about the relationship to the absolute *telos* we are talking about the relationship to God. We might even say that God is the ideal image of the self but not in the immediate sense.

> If God were in the immediate sense the ideal for human beings, it would be right to endeavor to express a direct likeness. Thus when a distinguished man is an ideal for me, it is quite proper for me to attempt to express a direct resemblance to him, since we are both human beings. . . . But as between God and a human being . . . there is an absolute difference. In man's absolute relationship to God this absolute difference must therefore come to expression, and any attempt to express an immediate likeness becomes impertinence. [*CUP*, 369]

Therefore, the only consistent expression of the absolute relation to the absolute *telos,* which is wholly other than every finite *telos,* is the continual renunciation of the claim to ultimacy of the latter.

In summary, we have seen that the existential task of becoming a self is the sustaining of an absolute relation to the absolute *telos,* and a relative relation to relative *teloi.* But the existential pathos arises because the individual finds himself in exactly the opposite situation. He is absolutely committed to relative ends and only relatively committed to the absolute *telos.* Thus, the initial expression of an absolute passion for the absolute is the resignation of all those finite ends in which he is entangled.

Suffering

Resignation is simply the *initial* expression of the existential pathos. The *essential* expression is suffering. Kierkegaard says,

> [To speak of] suffering as the essential expression for existential pathos means that suffering is real, . . . and by the reality of the suffering is meant its persistence as essential for the pathetic relationship to an external [sic] happiness.[2] [*CUP*, 396]

The suffering to which he refers is the concomitant of a passionate concern for selfhood. One cannot rid himself of this kind of suffering without renouncing the concern, and this is tantamount to renouncing his humanity.

Kierkegaard distinguishes several different responses to suffering. The aesthete deals with suffering as accidental and hence essentially unreal. There may be moments of existential despair; however, these are not moments of truth but untruth which will pass in time. "Aesthetically viewed." Kierkegaard writes, "suffering stands in an accidental relation to existence, it may indeed be there but it may also cease" (*CUP*, 400).

The ethicist, on the other hand, strives to alleviate the suffering through finite actualization of the infinite *telos*. This is ultimately impossible and the ironist knows it. The ironist is an ethicist incognito. He is an ethicist who "grasps the contradiction . . . between the manner in which he exists inwardly, and the fact that he does not outwardly express it" (*CUP*, 450). But neither the ethicist nor the ironist really comprehends the significance of the suffering.

The humorist comes closest to grasping its significance. He understands that suffering belongs to existence, "and that therefore all human beings suffer as long as they exist; . . . [he] does not identify suffering with misfortune, as if an existing individual would be happy if such and such misfortunes were not there" (*CUP*, 401). He "exists so that suffer-

2. The word should be "eternal."

ing is for him relevant to existence. But at that point the
humorist turns deceptively aside and revokes the suffering in
the form of a jest" (*CUP*, 400). He sees the discrepancy between the absolute *telos* and our ethical endeavors. He understands well the suffering of him who genuinely desires the
absolute but exists in the relative; but, instead of persisting in
the suffering mode of being, he relieves the suffering with a
jest.

Only the religious individual endures the suffering and refuses to accept a substitute for his absolute concern for the
absolute. Religious existence is not a way to alleviate suffering. On the contrary, it *is* suffering existence. The ultimate
suffering is what Kierkegaard calls *Anfaegtelese,* which his
English translators have preferred to leave in the German
equivalent, *Anfechtung. Anfechtung* is the limit which the
individual discovers in his quest for the absolute *telos.* It is
the temptation to flee from the eternal, the closer one
comes to it. It is the heightening dread which arises the
deeper one comprehends the cost of selfhood. Kierkegaard
elaborates.

> In the moment of the individual's success in training him-
> self for the absolute relationship through the renunciation
> of relative ends (and this may occur in particular moments,
> though the individual is again later drawn back into the
> conflict), and when he is now about to relate himself ab-
> solutely to the absolute, he discovers the limit, and the
> conflict of *Anfechtung* becomes an expression for this
> limit. [*CUP*, 411]

Thus we have in Kierkegaard a description of the way to
selfhood as a path of suffering, which begins with the com-
paratively easy suffering involved in renouncing the relative
ends in which one's life is dissipated, but which intensifies
with every step along the way and eventually reaches the limit
situation in which the cost becomes prohibitive.

Guilt-Consciousness

The decisive expression of existential pathos is guilt. Kierkegaard recapitulates as follows:

> [First] the task proposed was to relate oneself at the same time absolutely to the absolute *telos* and relatively to the relative ends. Just when a beginning ought to be made with this, it became evident that first of all immediacy must be overcome, or the individual must die from it, before there can be any question of realizing the task proposed.... [The next section] treated suffering as the essential expression of existential pathos, suffering regarded as dying from immediacy, suffering as the mark of the relationship of the exister to the absolute *telos*.... [And now] guilt is treated as the decisive expression for the existential pathos. [*CUP*, 468]

Kierkegaard concedes that this path might appear to be a backward movement. "And yet," he insists, "this backward movement is a forward movement, in so far as going forward means going deeper into something" (*CUP*, 469).

But how can the consciousness of guilt be considered to be the decisive expression for the relation of the individual to the absolute *telos*. The contrary would appear to be the case. One would assume that guilt is indicative of the fact that the individual is *not* related to the absolute *telos*. Kierkegaard's answer is that because it is a finite being who seeks the infinite, the relation will always be a disrelationship. Thus, the decisive evidence of the individual's passionate desire for the eternal is the consciousness of guilt. If this is lacking, then the individual is not related to the absolute *telos*.

This poses a more significant problem. Is guilt, so understood, really guilt? That is, is the individual really culpable for a guilt which is the consequence of his finitude?

> The fact that guilt is accounted for by existence seems to make the existor guiltless, it seems as though he could

throw the blame upon the one who has placed him in existence, or upon existence itself. In this case the consciousness of guilt would be nothing but a new expression for the suffering of existence. [*CUP*, 470]

Kierkegaard declares this line of thought self-contradictory. He argues that when a person protests his innocence in a particular situation he tacitly admits that essentially he is responsible for who he is—that he is guilty for who he has become.

He who totally or essentially is guiltless cannot be guilty in the particular instance; but he who is totally guilty can very well be innocent in the particular instance. So then, not only by being guilty in a particular instance does a man denounce himself as essentially guilty . . . but also by being innocent in the particular instance. [*CUP*, 471]

It is the consciousness of this *essential* guilt which is decisive for selfhood. One must choose to be guilty, as Kierkegaard puts it elsewhere, if he is to be a self, "for only when I choose myself as guilty do I choose myself absolutely" (*E/O*, II, 221). In short, in choosing to accept his essential guilt, the individual chooses selfhood. To insist upon his essential innocence is to renounce selfhood.

This guilt is not a relative guilt which arises from the relation of the individual to some relative *telos;* it is the sense of the totality of guilt which arises from the individual's relation to the absolute *telos.* Kierkegaard carefully distinguishes essential guilt from other forms of guilt. "Every conception of guilt is lower which does not by an eternal recollection put guilt together with the relation to an eternal happiness, but by memory puts it together with something lower, something comparative" (*CUP*, 481).

Kierkegaard observes that to every lower conception of guilt there is a corresponding satisfaction which is lower than that required of the essential consciousness of guilt. Every attempt to satisfy the consciousness of guilt through finitizing the guilt succeeds only in relativizing the *telos.* The civil conception of punishment, the metaphysical conception of nemesis, and even the religious conception of penance simply finitize the guilt and vitiate the individual's relation to the absolute *telos* by substituting for it some relative *telos.* Indeed, for the essential consciousness of guilt there is no finite satisfaction. So long as the absolute *telos* remains "wholly other," guilt-consciousness is the highest mode of being. It is only when the eternal enters time, when the abstract becomes concrete, that guilt is overcome and it is possible to begin the second movement in the restoration of selfhood—the movement of faith.

The Dialectical Factor

The state in which the absolute *telos* remains "wholly other" Kierkegaard calls "religiousness A," or the religion of immanence. "Religiousness B" breaks the immanental predicament and makes possible the completion of the therapeutic process. Religiousness A focuses on the therapeutic process without specifying the goal of therapy—the *telos* remains abstract, vaguely defined as the eternal. And so long as this remains the case, guilt-consciousness will be the most profound manifestation of selfhood possible.

In Religiousness B, however, the abstract *telos* becomes concrete; the eternal receives temporal specificity. The general *telos* of "selfhood" becomes the specific *telos* of "Christhood." Kierkegaard examines the effect this specificity has upon the existential pathos of the self.

Sin-Consciousness

The specification of the *telos* does not vitiate the existential pathos. On the contrary, it heightens it.

When a man existentially expresses and has expressed for a longer time that he gives up and has given up everything for the sake of the relationship to the absolute *telos,* the

circumstance that there are conditions has an absolute influence to develop in his passion the greatest possible tension. [*CUP*, 345]

Kierkegaard dramatically illustrates this with a parable which
must surely have been derived from his own childhood experience.

Think of a child, he says. Delight the child by showing him a
picture book of heroes in manly, courageous, and romantic
stance; but include the picture of a man upon a cross. No
doubt the child will wonder why you have included this
among the gallery of heroes and what this man did to deserve
such a cruel death. Kierkegaard counsels:

> Tell the child that He was love, that He came to the world
> out of love, took upon Him the form of a humble servant,
> lived only for one end, to love men and to help them,
> especially all those who were sick and sorrowful and suf-
> fering and unhappy. Then tell the child what befell Him in
> life, how one of the few that were close to Him betrayed
> Him, that the other few denied Him, and all the rest
> scoffed at and derided Him, until at last they nailed Him
> to the cross . . . whereas He prayed for them that this
> might not come to pass, that the heavenly Father would
> forgive them their fault. [*TiC*, 176]

What effect do you suppose this will have upon the child,
Kierkegaard asks. Surely the child will wonder why God allowed it to happen, why he did not destroy the men who dealt
thus with the loving One. With righteous indignation the child
resolves to avenge the death of such a holy One. But then in
time, perhaps, he may come to a different understanding of
the picture. He will no longer hate "the world in which they
spat upon the holy One, the world in which they crucify love
and beg acquittal for the robber" (*TiC*, 178), for in so doing
he would violate the One whom he has come to love. He will

only want to attain unto the likeness of Him who could forgive the men who crucified Him.

It should be apparent that such a specification of the absolute *telos* does not diminish the pathos of existence but accentuates it. The passion with which the individual has sought the *telos* of his life is heightened by this specificity. But by the same token the existential pathos which accompanies his nonbeing is intensified. The general pathos, guilt-consciousness, becomes specific and by virtue of this specificity becomes a heightened pathos. This is what Kierkegaard refers to as "the retroactive effect of the dialectical upon the pathetic" (*CUP*, 515).

More precisely, this sharpened pathos is sin-consciousness, a new mode of being. Prior to the faith response to the Christ event, guilt-consciousness characterizes the individual's mode of being; that is, the individual exists in the consciousness of his nonbeing. But this is an abstract sense of nonbeing. By faith this nonbeing becomes specific—the nonbeing of sin. Prior to faith the individual exists in the process of becoming, but it is merely a formal state. The individual is not becoming anything in particular. By faith, his becoming receives specificity. In Kierkegaard's words:

> Sin is the new existence medium. Apart from this, to exist means merely that the individual having come into the world is present and is in the process of becoming; now it means that having come into the world he has become a sinner; apart from this, "to exist" is not a more sharply defining predicate; one does not become anything in particular by coming into being, but now, to come into being is to become a sinner. In the totality of guilt-consciousness, existence asserts itself as strongly as it can within immanence; but sin-consciousness is the breach with immanence. [*CUP*, 516-17]

In short, guilt-consciousness is the most profound expression of the individual's sense of general nonbeing with respect to his own immanental yearning for eternal happiness; sin-consciousness is the consciousness of a specific nonbeing with respect to a definitive mode of being which stands over against him.

Forgiveness of Sin

At this point a critical juncture in the quest for selfhood has been reached. The consuming passion for selfhood has led the individual to renounce the claim to ultimacy of every relative *telos*. The path of resignation has led through suffering to guilt-consciousness. Here, in Christ, one discovers his *telos*—the mode of being which claims to be the true goal of human existence. Confronted with this image of selfhood, the general sense of nonbeing becomes specific. But clarity with respect to the *telos* of human being, and the conviction of one's own nonbeing with respect to this *telos* are not equivalent to existing in the new mode of being. Sin-consciousness alone cannot generate the new being in us. What Kierkegaard might have termed "grace-consciousness" is essential. Coincident with the consciousness of sin must be the acceptance of the forgiveness of sin, the acceptance of the grace which is extended to us in our nonbeing.

The notion of the forgiveness of sin is an offense against reason. Deep as the desire may be to be forgiven one's nonbeing, it is not reasonable to suppose that nonbeing can be "forgiven" at all, to say nothing of the audacity of the claim that a *man* could forgive nonbeing. As Kierkegaard expresses it elsewhere,

> The Jews were quite right in being offended at Christ because he would forgive sins. It requires a singularly high degree of dullness . . . not to be offended at the fact that a man would forgive sins. And in the next place it requires an equally singular degree of dullness not to be offended at the assertion that sin can be forgiven. This is for the hu-

man understanding the most impossible thing of all. [*SuD*, 247]

Hence, reason can never bring a man to accept the forgiveness of sin for forgiveness is a paradox, an offense against reason.

In the *Postscript*, Kierkegaard explains the paradoxicality of the doctrine of the forgiveness of sin.

> Forgiveness is a paradox . . . because the existing individual is stamped as a sinner, by which existence is accentuated a second time, and because it purports to be an eternal decision in time with retroactive power to annul the past, and because it is linked with the existence of God in time. [*CUP*, 201]

Thus the doctrine of the forgiveness of sin is offensive to the understanding on three counts. First, it implies that by coming into existence the individual has become a sinner. Second, it presupposes that the past can be annulled. And third, it rests upon the assumption that the eternal entered time. All three suppositions are incomprehensible to reason. Reason would maintain that being is not tantamount to nonbeing; that the past is irrevocable; and that the eternal, by definition, cannot be temporal. Reason cannot resolve the paradox and arrive at the forgiveness of sin. The forgiveness of sin is not an objective principle to be appropriated by reason; it is a subjective attitude to be appropriated by faith. Only he who despairs of reason as the way to salvation can appropriate forgiveness. Kierkegaard concludes:

> The individual existing human being must feel himself a sinner; not objectively, which is nonsense, but subjectively, which is the most profound suffering. With all the strength of his mind, to the last thought, . . . he must try to understand the forgiveness of sins, and then despair of the understanding. With the understanding directly opposed to it, the inwardness of faith must lay hold of the paradox; and

precisely this struggle on the part of faith . . . constitutes
the tension of its inwardness. [*CUP,* 201]

In the end we are pushed back to the fundamental paradox
of the Christian faith, Jesus Christ. In Christ we are confronted
with a *telos* the authenticity of which is grounded not in rea-
soned argument but in the existential impact of a life. Christ
draws men to himself. This evocative mode of salvation takes
seriously what it means to be a self and indeed requires the self
to be a self.

> The phrase 'to draw truly to oneself,' cannot mean merely
> to draw it away from being its own self, to draw it in such
> a way that it loses its own existence by being drawn into
> that which draws it unto itself. . . . No, when that which is
> to be drawn is in itself a self, the real meaning of truly
> drawing to oneself is, first to help it to become truly its
> own self, so as then to draw it to oneself, or it means to
> help it to become its own self with and by the drawing of
> it to oneself. [*TiC,* 159]

The Christian therapeutic, then, is a composite act which involves both the evocative power of the Self which makes a
claim upon us, and the free response of the self which is thereby called into being.

> That which can be said truly to draw to *itself,* must first of
> all be something in itself. . . . That which can be said truly
> to draw to itself must be the higher, the nobler, which
> draws up the lower to itself. . . . But a self can be truly
> drawn to another only through a choice, so that 'truly
> drawing to oneself' is a composite act. . . . He would draw
> him only as a free being, and so through a choice. [*TiC,*
> 158ff.]

The self, to be a self, must risk itself. The only certainty is the
certitude of faith. "Only eternity can give an eternal certainty," Kierkegaard points out, "while existence must rest

content with a militant certainty, a certainty not achieved by the struggle becoming weaker, and in fact illusory, but only by its becoming stronger" (*CUP*, 203).

Existence in Faith

Thus, Christian existence is a dialectical existence—an existence which moves between the poles of sin and grace, of dread and faith. The drama of suffering love can move us to identify ourselves with his self, but it does not follow that we then become "Christs." No, it merely follows that we become Christians—thrust into the dialectic of becoming who we are drawn by him to be. By his forgiveness we are convicted and brought to a consciousness of our sin. Yet we are also drawn toward him and his mode of being. By his forgiving love we are enabled to transcend our past, to become who by faith we are.

This is the "education by dread" of which Kierkegaard writes, the "training in Christianity." Jesus Christ is the finite actuality which is the source of our faith. Yet he is also the infinite possibility of human being, the prospect of which fills us with dread. "This dread," Kierkegaard says, "is by the aid of faith absolutely educative, consuming as it does all finite aims and discovering all their deceptions" (*CoD*, 139). He continues,

> But in order that the individual may thus absolutely and infinitely be educated by possibility, he must be honest towards possibility and must have faith. . . . If at the beginning of his education he misunderstands the anguish of dread, so that it does not lead him to faith but away from faith, then he is lost. . . . With the help of faith dread trains the individual to find repose in providence. [*CoD*, 140, 142, 144]

In *Training in Christianity*, Kierkegaard gives concretion to this abstract description of Christian becoming. Again, the illustration is surely autobiographical. Kierkegaard asks us to think of a young man who has been drawn by the One who was perfect love. The man is utterly committed to this image of selfhood. He desires to be transformed into his image. He even begins to resemble him. And then suddenly he discovers an environment of reality in which he is placed and the relation of this environment to him. Kierkegaard says to this young man:

> Now life's seriousness begins for thee, now thou hast come so far out that thou canst take seriously the notion that to live is to take an examination. For life's seriousness does not consist in all this busyness about business and temporal things, about livelihood and employment and place-finding and the procreation of children, but life's seriousness consists in the *will* to be and to express perfection in everyday reality. [*TiC,* 188]

Standing there in his real world, the young man knows the meaning of dread for he can glimpse what this love will cost him. But he does not let go of the image he has come to love. Instead he faces the suffering to which it has led him.

> He holds out, and by thus holding out he is strengthened, as one is strengthened by suffering—now he loves doubly that picture of perfection, for what one suffers for, one loves more dearly. . . . No help came in the way he had hoped; only in an entirely different sense has he been helped, for he has become stronger. [*TiC,* 189]

Thus it is that *governance,* to use Kierkegaard's term, helps the Christian. It leads him farther and farther into suffering, because he will not let go of that image which he desires to resemble. Kierkegaard pushes this to the very limit. Suppose, he says, that at the bitterest moment the Christian is deserted by his last support—by God. Suppose that even then he chooses not to let go of this image, because, as he says, "I can do no other." Suppose that he holds out unto the last, even unto death. "Thus," Kierkegaard concludes, "he stood his test, became and continued to be a Christian, drawn by Him who from on high will draw all unto Himself" (*TiC,* 193).

8. Freud's Concept of Psychotherapy

The Inception of the Psychoanalytic Method

As his therapeutic method developed, Freud's theories were continually in flux. He was constantly experimenting and making innovations. While engaged with Joseph Breuer in the "cathartic" method of therapy, Freud was also still employing the physical methods of electrotherapy, massage, baths, and so forth. And when he collaborated with Breuer in publishing the results of their work, he was already introducing modifications which foreshadowed the development of the psychoanalytic method. Still, it is possible to discern the direction of the evolution of his therapeutic theory. Coincident with his shift in perspective from the physiological to the psychological to the metapsychological, there is a shift in his understanding of the locus of the therapeutic problem from the neurological to the psychological and, within the psychological, from the gnoseological to the volitional. This shift in the understanding of the problem's nature necessitates a shift in therapeutic method from physiological therapy to psychotherapy and, within the latter, from "recollection" to "repetition."

A brief review of Freud's early therapeutic methods should be helpful before we turn to the crucial problems, resistance and transference, which led to the development of the psychoanalytic method.

Freud's interest in psychotherapy can be traced to his hearing about Breuer's curious case of Anna O. Prior to this, his field of specialization had been neurology; the case marked the beginning of a change in his interest from the physiological to the psychological. A classic case of hysteria, Anna suffered from a plethora of symptoms including paralysis in three limbs and visual and speech disturbances. Breuer was unable to help her, until on one occasion she related the details of the first appearance of a particular symptom. To Breuer's surprise this resulted in the symptom's complete disappearance. Subsequent discussion of other symptoms met with the same result (*SiH*, 14-31). Freud heard about the case shortly after its termination. What fascinated him was the obvious implication that hysterical symptoms were not solely attributable to physiological causes but had a psychogenesis. Nevertheless, it was seven years before he returned to the method Breuer had stumbled upon.

Freud spent the better part of the next two years in clinical neurology under Dr. Meynert in Vienna. He then received a postgraduate stipend which made possible a year of study in Paris with Charcot, one of the greatest names in neurology. Freud looked forward to discussing Breuer's remarkable discovery with Charcot, and, though Charcot's response was not enthusiastic, his relationship with Freud contributed to the latter's developing interest in psychotherapy. What impressed Freud the most was Charcot's demonstration of the psychogenic origin of certain hysterical symptoms. Freud reported,

> While he was occupied with the study of hysterical paralysis appearing after traumas, the idea occurred to him to reproduce by artificial means such paralyses as he had previously carefully differentiated from organic disturbances; for this purpose he took hysterical patients and placed them in a state of somnambulism by hypnotism. He succeeded in producing a faultless demonstration and proved thereby that these paralyses were the result of specific ideas holding sway in the brain of the patient. [*CP*, I, 22]

Thus the insight Freud had gained from Breuer's earlier discovery was confirmed. The implication was that, since the symptoms resulted from the persistence of certain ideas in the mind, they could be treated by counter ideas.

Nevertheless, upon returning to Vienna Freud did not immediately employ Breuer's "talking cure." In his first therapeutic efforts he used the conventional method of electrotherapy but was utterly frustrated with the results. Disillusioned with this method, Freud turned to the more promising one, hypnotic suggestion, which was being employed by Bernheim in Nancy. He even translated Bernheim's book into German, contributing a significant preface of his own. Here he noted,

> All phenomena of hypnotism have the same origin: they arise, that is from a suggestion, a conscious idea, which had been introduced into the brain of the hypnotized person by an external influence and has been accepted by him as though it had arisen spontaneously. [*CP*, V, 14]

Consequently, hypnotic suggestion is seen to have therapeutic potential as a suitable method for combating certain nervous disorders whose symptoms are psychogenic.

A few years later Freud published an account of a case he has successfully treated by hypnosis (*CP*, V, 33-46). In his theoretical interpretation of the psychical mechanism of hysteria, Freud employed the concept of "antithetic ideas"—ideas which inhibit the individual's conscious intentions in somatic ways. Freud overcame the debilitating symptoms through hypnotic suggestion. But the success he enjoyed with this treatment was only temporary; the identical symptoms returned thus necessitating repetition of the hypnotic suggestion. Freud soon turned to other methods. In an essay entitled "On Psychotherapy" he told why.

> I gave up the suggestive technique, and with it hypnosis, so early in my practice because I despaired of making suggestion powerful and enduring enough to effect permanent

cures. In all severe cases I saw the suggestions which had been applied crumble away again; and then the disease or some substitute for it returned. [*CP*, I, 254]

Still intrigued with Breuer's discovery of the remarkable remission which followed the recollection of events coincident to the first appearance of symptoms, Freud turned to the "talking cure." The first case, begun on May 1, 1889, in which he employed the cathartic method was that of Emmy von N. But Freud was still dependent upon suggestion, combined with massage, baths, and rest. Over the next several years in association with Breuer, he continued to explore the possibilities of the cathartic method, and in 1893 they published the results of their clinical studies. Here they described the method:

> In the great majority of cases it is impossible to discover this starting-point by straight-forward interrogation of the patient, be it ever so thorough . . . because it is often a matter of experiences which the patient finds it disagreeable to discuss. . . . As a rule it is necessary to hypnotize the patient and under hypnosis to arouse recollections relating to the time when the symptom first appeared. [*CP*, I, 24]

The intent of the therapy is to bring into clear recollection the traumatic event and the accompanying emotions. When the patient has expressed his feelings about the event in words, the hysterical symptoms disappear.

Three years later Freud published an essay that was extremely critical of the cathartic method. He noted, "It does not influence the casual determinations of hysteria, and hence, it cannot prevent the origin of new symptoms in the place of those removed" (*SiH*, 195). This is a most serious indictment of the method. The treatment does not really get at the root of the problem; it is a symptomatic, not a causal, treatment. Freud also discovered that some patients could not be hypnotized and, since it is necessary to "broaden the consciousness" in order to disclose the pathogenic experiences, he was forced to seek another method.

One case he found particularly instructive was that of Lucie R. He wrote, "On attempting to hypnotize Miss Lucie R., she did not lapse into the somnambulic state. I, therefore, was obliged to forego somnambulism, and the analysis was made while she was in a state which did not perhaps differ much from the normal" (*SiH*, 78). What encouraged Freud to persist in the face of this obstacle was a demonstration Bernheim had performed to prove that things experienced under hypnosis are only apparently forgotten in the waking state and can be recalled when the subject is urged to do so. Perceiving a similarity between the hypnotic state and the pathological condition, Freud said, "I decided to proceed on the supposition that my patients knew everything that was of any pathogenic significance, and that all that was necessary was to force them to impart it" (*SiH*, 79). Following Bernheim's example, whenever he came to a point where the patient claimed to have no recollection concerning the origin of some particular symptom, he assured her that she did know it and urged her to recall it. The recollection usually followed. In this way the analysis proceeded without the necessity of hypnotism.

This shift from hypnotically induced recollection to the "concentration technique" marked the beginning of the free association method of therapy. Freud continued to employ urging and direct questioning for some time, but the method left something to be desired. "One cannot go very far with such simple assurances as, 'You do know it, just say it,' or 'It will soon come to your mind.' After a few sentences the thread breaks even in the patient who is in a state of concentration" (*SiH*, 202). Experience taught Freud that the relaxation of censorship is the key to recollection. This conviction enabled him gradually to relinquish all his probing techniques. Increasingly he allowed the analysis to take its own course, until at last the free association method became truly free.

The chain of associations leads inevitably to an event in the patient's personal history of sufficient traumatic quality and power to be determinative of his behavior (*CP*, I, 186). If the event so discovered does not appear to fulfill these specifications, we may be sure that the path must be pursued further (*CP*, I, 188). In fact, Freud discovered that

> the patient's associations led back from the scene which one was trying to elucidate to earlier experiences, and compelled analysis . . . to occupy itself with the past. This regression led constantly further backwards; at first it seemed regularly to bring us to puberty; later on . . . still further back into years of childhood. . . . It appeared that psycho-analysis could explain nothing current without referring back to something past; more, that every pathogenic experience implied a previous one, which, though not in itself pathogenic, had yet endowed the later one with its pathogenic quality. [*CP*, I, 290-91]

There is here a kind of infinite regression which encompasses, in principle at least, the subject's entire personal history.

The Problem of Resistance

It is apparent that there had taken place a subtle shift in the focus of the therapeutic problem. Whereas at first the therapeutic problem was to bring to light the particular traumatic event which precipitated the outbreak of the neurosis, the focus was subsequently widened to include the whole complex of historical experience which gives an event its traumatic impact. There developed a second, and even more radical, major shift in Freud's understanding of the therapeutic problem. This was the shift from the gnoseological to the volitional. Freud acknowledged this shift in an address delivered before the Second International Psycho-Analytical Congress at Nuremberg in 1910.

> You know that our technique has been transformed in important respects. At the time of the cathartic treatment

we set ourselves the aim of elucidating the symptoms, then we turned away from the symptoms to discovering the 'complexes', to use Jung's indispensable word; now, however, our work is aimed directly at finding out and overcoming the 'resistances', and we can with justification rely on the complexes coming to light as soon as the resistances have been recognized and removed. [*CP,* II, 288]

This shift in the locus of the therapeutic problem was not a renunciation of the earlier concern but a successive deepening of Freud's understanding of the task of therapy. He was still concerned with recollection, but what was sought in the recollecting and how this recollection was made possible was now the question. The first shift represents a deeper understanding of the complexity of that which is to be recollected. The second represents a deeper understanding of the complexity of the process of recollection. The problem is seen to be not so much ignorance as it is that which brought about and sustains the ignorance. In short, the problem is fundamentally more one of willing than of knowing.

This shift in Freud's understanding of the locus of the therapeutic problem arose out of his clinical experience. In the practice of his free association method of therapy, Freud discovered that the flow of associated ideas inevitably came to a halt before reaching the significant level of recollection. The patient abruptly changed the subject or blocked up entirely professing a genuine amnesia, a void of ideas or memories. This was highly frustrating to the therapeutic progress, but Freud took it to be significant. He interpreted these interruptions in the flow of associations as psychic resistance to recollection which performs a definite psychic function. He was convinced that this block is a psychic defense against some painful recollection.

Perhaps the earliest recognition of the psychic resistances preventing recollection was Freud's reference to *antithetic ideas.* He distinguished two kinds of ideas: intentions and expectations. The response to certain intentions is an anxious expectation. This functions in opposition to the intention; it functions as an antithetic idea. The normal individual manages to circumvent such antithetic ideas and to act on his intention, or he does so only in a greatly modified way. His will is virtually paralyzed. "The antithetic idea establishes itself, so to speak, as a *'counter-will'*, while the patient is aware with astonishment of having a will which is resolute but powerless" (*CP*, V, 40).

This is the first indication that Freud understood the problem to be more one of will than of knowledge. He gave a vivid description of the debilitating effect of such antithetic ideas:

> This emergence of a counter-will is chiefly responsible for the characteristic which often gives to hysterics the appearance almost of being possessed by an evil spirit—the characteristic, that is, of not being able to do something precisely at the moment when they want to most passionately, of doing the exact opposite of what they have been asked to do, and of being obliged to cover what they most value with abuse and contempt. . . . Compulsions such as these . . . may often affect the most irreproachable characters when for a time they become the helpless victims of their antithetic ideas. [*CP*, V, 44]

Freud concluded that the resistances which his therapeutic efforts encountered were produced by the same forces which created the repression in the first place. An examination of his clinical data revealed that the repressed pathogenic ideas were of a character which provoked feelings of psychic pain, of shame, guilt, and anxiety; feelings which one would understandably prefer to forget. Hence, the patient's ego constructed a defense against the unbearable idea. It "forgot" the idea and the event which evoked it. To be sure, the affect was not obliterated; it was simply repressed. It persisted beneath the threshold of consciousness thus requiring the continued ego defense. When the free flow of associated ideas approached the sensitive area of the memory, the same force which originally expelled the idea from consciousness was encountered as a resistance to recollection. Freud concluded,

> Hence, a psychic force, the repugnance of the ego, has originally crowded the pathogenic idea from the association, and now opposed its return into the memory. The not knowing of the hysterics was really a—more or less conscious—not willing to know, and the task of the therapist was to overpower this association resistance by psychic labor. [*SiH*, 202]

In a later essay on technique, Freud explained how he arrived at this insight. He told about a case of hysteria in which the mother of a girl who was his patient confided to him the homosexual experience which had precipitated the attacks. The girl had completely forgotten the event. Freud, acting on the theory that knowledge is therapeutic, repeated the mother's story to the girl. Each time he did so the girl reacted with an hysterical attack, after which the story was immediately forgotten again.

> There was no doubt that the patient was expressing a violent resistance against the knowledge which was being forced upon her; at last she simulated imbecility and total loss of memory in order to defend herself against what I told her. After this, there was no alternative but to abandon the previous attribution of importance to knowledge in itself, and to lay the stress upon the resistances which had originally induced the condition of ignorance and were still now prepared to defend it. Conscious knowledge, even if it were not again expelled, was powerless against those resistances. [*CP*, II, 363]

Thus the pathological factor is not ignorance per se but the inner resistances which inaugurated, and continue to sustain, the ignorance. Combating these resistances becomes the crucial task of therapy (*CP*, II, 302).

Indeed, this is the fundamental reason Freud gave up hypnosis as a therapeutic method—"it conceals from us all insight into the play of mental forces" (*CP,* I, 254). It obscures the recognition of the resistance by means of which the patient clings to his neurosis and even struggles against his own recovery. And yet only by means of this phenomenon can we comprehend his bizarre behavior. "Hypnosis does not do away with the resistance but only avoids it and therefore yields only incomplete information and transitory therapeutic success" (*CP,* I, 269). In fact, in his "History of the Psycho-Analytic Movement" Freud dated the origin of psychoanalysis proper from the shift in the focus of the therapeutic interest from trauma to resistance—from knowing to willing.

This therapy is still concerned with the patient's personal history, but the emphasis is not so much on knowing as on comprehending. And the method has shifted from informing the patient to undoing the resistances so that he may comprehend what he already knows. It is still important to lift up the unconscious ideas and feelings into consciousness since, as Freud says, "conscious will-power governs only the conscious mental processes, and every mental compulsion is rooted in the unconscious" (*CP,* I, 261). But the method is the overcoming of the resistance which functions dynamically to keep these painful ideas from conscious recognition.

> The discovery of the unconscious and the introduction of it into consciousness is performed in the face of a continuous *resistance* on the part of the patient. The process of bringing this unconscious material to light is associated with 'pain' *(Unlust),* and because of this pain the patient again and again rejects it. . . . If you succeed in persuading him to accept, by virtue of a better understanding, something that up to now, in consequence of this automatic regulation by pain, he has rejected (repressed), you will then have accomplished something towards his education. . . . Psycho-analytic treatment may in general be con-

ceived of as such a *re-education in overcoming internal resistances.* [*CP*, I, 261-62]

Thus the therapeutic process involves suffering. It requires that the individual learn to confront anxiety. It requires the re-education of the ego.

The Transference Phenomenon

A concomitant of the shift in Freud's understanding of the locus of the therapeutic problem was a shift in his therapeutic method. When the problem was understood to be one of knowing, certain methods of therapy seemed appropriate. But when it became apparent that the problem was far more complex, that there was operative here a kind of will to ignorance, a new therapeutic method was required. Hypnotic suggestion was seen to be a temporary expedient and the carthartic method superficial. Even the method of free association simply served to reveal the existence of a strong countervailing force. In fact, the closer the patient gets to the critical area, the more anxious he becomes and the more compulsive his resistance becomes to the recollection of this crucial segment of his past.

It became clear to Freud that it is the physician's task to create motives for overcoming the resistance. And with this recognition there came a shift in the character of the therapeutic relationship between patient and physician—a shift from a fundamentally objective relation to a more and more subjective one. Taking inventory of the resources available for overcoming the resistance, Freud focused his attention upon two: the intellectual interest of the patient, and his affective relationship with the therapist. Freud was always aware of the importance of each, but over the years a shift of emphasis from one to the other took place.

Capitalizing upon the former, Freud introduced the notion of *interpretation.*

On explaining and imparting to him [the patient] the

knowledge of the marvelous world of psychic processes, which we have gained only through such analysis, we obtain his collaboration and cause him to view himself with the objective interest of the investigator, and thus we drive back the resistance which rests on an affective basis. [*SiH*, 213]

To be sure, this impartation of knowledge is not on the same level as that to which I referred earlier. Formerly, communication concerned the traumatic event itself, some forgotten memory the knowledge of which was supposed to bring freedom from the neurotic symptoms. Here Freud means the impartation of an understanding of the psychic processes at work in the individual. He feels that this kind of information will excite the patient's interest, provide him with a certain objectivity toward himself, and secure his continued interest and collaboration in the analytic process.

This basically objective role of the analyst as one who imparts information, gradually gave way to the more subjective role of interpreter. And psychoanalysis became more the art of interpretation, and less the teaching of an ideology. Freud described this art well in an encyclopedia article.

Experience soon showed that the attitude which the analytical physician could most advantageously adopt was to surrender himself to his own unconscious mental activity, in a state of *easy and impartial attention,* to avoid so far as possible reflection and the construction of conscious expectations, not to try to fix anything that he heard particularly in his memory, and by these means to catch the drift of the patient's unconscious with his own unconscious. It was then found that, except under conditions that were too unfavourable, the patient's associations emerged like allusions, as it were, to one particular theme and that it was only necessary for the physician to go a step further in order to guess the material which was concealed from the patient himself and to be able to communicate it to him. It is true that this work of interpretation was not to be brought under strict rules and left a great deal of play to the physician's tact and skill; but, with impartiality and practice, it was usually possible to obtain trustworthy results. [*CP*, V, 112]

There is here an unmistakable shift in the direction of subjectivity. The method suggested requires a high degree of subjectivity from the therapist.

The art of interpretation, however, does more to illuminate the therapist's understanding of the problem than it does the patient's. Freud noted, "After the analyst's curiosity had, as it were, been gratified by the elaboration of the technique of interpretation, it was inevitable that interest should turn to the problem of discovering the most effective way of influencing the patient" (*CP*, V, 124). Reviewing more than twenty-five years of therapeutic work, Freud wrote,

At first the analysing physician could do no more than discover the unconscious material that was concealed from the patient, put it together, and, at the right moment, communicate it to him. Psycho-analysis was then first and foremost an art of interpreting. Since this did not solve the therapeutic problem a further aim quickly came in view: to oblige the patient to confirm the analyst's construction from his own memory. In that endeavour the chief emphasis lay upon the patient's resistances: the art consisted now in uncovering these as quickly as possible, in pointing them out to the patient and in inducing him by human influence . . . to abandon his resistances. [*BPP*, 38]

This is not to say that the art of interpretation no longer has a place in therapy but simply that it is contingent upon a more fundamental factor, the patient's relationship to the therapist and the influence which the therapist's own person exercises upon the patient. Freud treated this relationship under the category of *transference*.

As early as 1895 Freud was aware of the "important role falling to the personality of the physician in the creation of motives which are to overcome the psychic force of resistance" (*SiH,* 299). He explained, "If this relation of the patient to the physician is disturbed, the readiness of the patient's collaboration fails" (*SiH,* 299). If the patient feels personally estranged from the physician through any real or fancied slight or disparagement, if the patient fears the loss of his identity through becoming too dependent on the physician, or if the patient is anxious lest certain long-repressed feelings become directed toward the physician, the collaboration and cooperation of the patient is jeopardized (*SiH,* 299-300).

Thus, while interpretation and instruction are important, they will not be effective until a strong rapport is established with the patient by means of which he may be induced to appropriate the interpretation. "When shall we begin our disclosures to the patient?" Freud asked. His answer: "Not until a dependable transference, a well-developed *rapport* is established in the patient" (*CP,* II, 360). And how is this rapport established?

> To ensure this one need do nothing but allow him [the patient] time. If one devotes serious interest in him, clears away carefully the first resistances that arise and avoids certain mistakes, such an attachment develops in the patient of itself, and the physician becomes linked up with one of the images of those persons from whom he was used to receive kindness. [*CP,* II, 360]

Freud cautioned that "it is certainly possible to forfeit this primary success if one takes up from the start any standpoint other than that of understanding, such as a moralizing attitude" (*CP,* II, 360).

> Hence it follows that the new sources of strength for which the sufferer is indebted to the analyst resolve them-

selves into transference, and instruction. . . . The patient
only makes use of the instruction, however, in so far as he
is induced to do so by the transference; and therefore until
a powerful transference is established the first explanation
should be withheld; and likewise, we may add, with each
subsequent one, we must wait until each disturbance of
the transference by the transference-resistance arising in
succession has been removed. [*CP*, II, 365]

It was not long, however, until it became apparent that the
transference phenomenon was not always conducive to therapy. In a paper entitled "The Dynamics of the Transference,"
Freud noted that whereas the transference to the therapist of
attitudes of confidence and trust—which had been learned in
the patient's earliest parental relationships—facilitated the
appropriation of the therapist's interpretation of the dynamics
of his illness, the process often worked in reverse. That is,

When there is anything in the complex material (the content of the complex) which can at all suitably be transferred on to the person of the physician such a transference will be effected . . . ; it will then manifest itself by the
signs of resistance—for instance, a cessation in the flow of
associations. [*CP*, II, 317]

This of course frustrates the therapeutic process.

Freud interpreted this contradictory phenomena by means
of a distinction between positive transference, the transference
of affectionate feeling, and negative transference, the transference of hostile feeling (*CP*, II, 319). The former facilitates
analysis; the latter produces the resistance. The therapist
should seek, therefore, to dissociate the negative components
of the emotional relationship from himself, while sustaining
the positive components of the transference in order to en-
hance the therapeutic progress (*CP*, II, 319). Freud concluded
that it is precisely this positive transference of affect to the
therapist which makes it possible for the patient to appro-

priate the therapist's interpretation of the dynamics of his illness and thereby gain freedom from it.

> The results of psycho-analysis rest upon a basis of suggestion; only by suggestion we must be understood to mean . . . influence on a person through and by means of the transference-manifestations of which he is capable. The eventual independence of the patient is our ultimate object when we use suggestion to bring him to carry out a mental operation that will necessarily result in a lasting improvement in his mental condition. [*CP*, II, 319-20]

The other side of the problem of transference in the therapeutic process is the continual danger of counter transference. Freud recognized that the physician is not immune to the same psychic processes which he recognizes are at work in his patient. Just as the patient may transfer to the physician emotions appropriate to a relationship experienced in his distant past, so the patient may influence the unconscious feelings of the physician so that he responds to the patient in ways appropriate to his own early relationships. Hence, "every analyst's achievement is limited by what his own complexes and resistance permit." Freud concluded, "Consequently we require that he should begin his practice with a self-analysis and should extend and deepen this constantly while making his observations on his patients" (*CP*, II, 289).

Again we must note the amazing shift that has taken place in Freud's therapeutic practice with respect to the character of the relationship between the patient and the physician. Beginning from a position of studied objectivity on the part of the physician, with only slight awareness of the importance of the physician's personal influence upon the patient, Freud moved to an intensely subjective relationship between the physician and the patient, but not, we must remember, to the point of jeopardizing the identity of either.

Recollection, Repetition, and Working Through

Just as the shift in Freud's understanding of the therapeutic problem necessitated a shift in therapeutic method, so the shift in methodology brought a new understanding of the therapeutic process. In a paper entitled "Recollection, Repetition and Working Through," Freud set forth the dynamics of therapy. In his characteristic manner, he began by reviewing the evolution of the psychoanalytic method with respect to the goals of therapy.

> Its first phase was that of Breuer's catharsis, direct concentration upon the events exciting symptom-formation and persistent efforts on this principle to obtain reproduction of the mental processes involved in that situation, in order to bring about a release of them through conscious operations. The aims pursued at that time, by the help of the hypnotic condition, were 'recollection' and 'abreaction'. Next, after hypnosis had been abandoned, the main task became that of divining from the patient's free associations what he failed to remember. Resistances were to be circumvented by the work of interpretation and by making its results known to the patient; concentration on the situations giving rise to symptom-formation and on those which lay behind the outbreak of illness was retained. . . . Finally, the present-day technique evolved itself, whereby the analyst abandons concentration on any particular element or problem, contents himself with studying whatever is occupying the patient's mind at the moment, and employs the art of interpretation mainly for the purpose of recognizing the resistances which come up in regard to this material and making the patient aware of them. [*CP,* II, 366-67]

Freud added, "The aim of these different procedures has of course remained the same throughout: descriptively, to recover the lost memories; dynamically, to conquer the resistances caused by repression" (*CP*, II, 367). But it is often impossible for the patient to remember that which is most essential. Even when the therapist has been able to discern and reconstruct the repressed material, the patient is often unable to appropriate it. While he may have intellectually understood the physician's interpretation of the dynamics of his problem, he has not emotionally comprehended its significance. In short, the aim which has been set up is not attained. Freud was forced to seek another means to accomplish this end.

At this point Freud made a significant discovery. He noted that while "the patient *remembers* nothing of what is forgotten and repressed," he often "expresses it in *action*" (*CP*, II, 369). Freud called this the *repetition compulsion,* since "he [the patient] reproduces it not in his memory but in his behavior; he *repeats* it, without of course knowing that he is repeating it" (*CP*, II, 369).

> For instance, the patient does not say that he remembers how defiant and critical he used to be in regard to the authority of his parents, but he behaves in that way towards the physician. He does not remember how he came to a helpless and hopeless deadlock in his infantile searchings after the truth of sexual matters, but he produces a mass of confused dreams and associations, complains that he never succeeds at anything, and describes it as his fate never to be able to carry anything through. He does not remember that he was intensely ashamed of certain sexual activities, but he makes it clear that he is ashamed of the treatment to which he has submitted himself, and does his utmost to keep it a secret; and so on. [*CP*, II, 369]

The compulsion to repeat the relationship patterns of one's early life is not limited to neurotics, as Freud later observed. It can be seen functioning in the lives of people who otherwise give no indication of neurosis. They seem to be demon possessed or driven by some malevolent fate. But this fate, Freud insisted, is one which is arranged by themselves through their response to their early infantile experiences. He declared, "The compulsion which is here in evidence differs in no way from the compulsion to repeat which we have found in neurotics, even though the people we are now considering have never shown any signs of dealing with a neurotic conflict by producing symptoms" (*BPP*, 44).

Perhaps the keenest insight of all Freud's discoveries about the dynamics of the human mind is his conclusion that the compulsion to repeat is the patient's way of remembering, and that as such it can be utilized in the therapeutic process. The repetition becomes a kind of existential recollection, and, since recollection is essential to a successful therapy, the repetition can be used as a therapeutic tool.

Actually, the repetition compulsion is a manifestation of the transference phenomenon. It is, Freud says, "the transference of the forgotten past not only on to the physician, but also on to all the other aspects of the current situation" (*CP*, II, 370). And, even as the transference phenomenon may manifest itself as a mode of resistance to therapeutic progress, so the compulsion to repeat may be an expression of resistance. In hypnotic therapy, Freud points out, all resistance is abrogated and the recollection is ideal. Under the methods of psychoanalysis the recollection is also successful so long as it is carried out under the conditions of a mild, positive transference. But if "as the analysis proceeds, this transference becomes hostile . . . necessitating repression, remembering immediately gives way to expression in action" (*CP*, II, 370-71). The individual falls back upon earlier immature ways of responding to a difficult situation. He becomes the victim of the compulsion to repeat. In effect, "the past is the patient's armory out of which he fetches his weapons for defending himself against the progress of analysis" (*CP*, II, 371).

Freud took this not as a defeat but as an opportunity for a more comprehensive understanding of the dynamics of the individual's psychic life. Compared with the skeletal recollection which is recovered in verbal discourse, this recollection is full-bodied, dynamic.

> Causing memories to be revived under hypnosis gives the impression of an experiment in the laboratory. Allowing 'repetition' during analytic treatment, which is the latest form of technique, constitutes a conjuring into existence of a piece of real life. [*CP*, II, 371]

So Freud permitted, even encouraged, the repetition of the patient's neurotic mode of relating to others—in this case, Freud himself—in order to help the patient understand the dynamics of his sickness in the context of his current experiences. By permitting himself to be drawn into the psychic drama of the patient's neurotic repetition compulsion Freud was "replacing his [the patient's] whole ordinary neurosis by a 'transference-neurosis' of which he can be cured by the therapeutic work" (*CP*, II, 374). Freud continued:

> The transference thus forms a kind of intermediary realm between illness and real life, through which the journey from the one to the other must be made. The new state of mind has absorbed all the features of the illness; it represents, however, an artificial illness which is at every point accessible to our interventions. It is at the same time a piece of real life, but adapted to our purposes by specially favourable conditions, and it is of a provisional character. [*CP*, II, 374-75]

This substitute transference neurosis provides contemporary, dramatic data with which to work. It is a limited neurosis which can be kept under control and by means of which the physician can enable the patient to gain the insight and conviction concerning the dynamics of his own peculiar self which were not possible under the limitations of verbal recollection. In *Beyond the Pleasure Principle,* Freud briefly summarized the physician's task:

The physician cannot as a rule spare his patient this phase of the treatment. He must get him to re-experience some portion of his forgotten life, but must see to it, on the other hand, that the patient retains some degree of aloofness, which will enable him, in spite of everything, to recognize that what appears to be reality is in fact only a reflection of a forgotten past. If this can be successfully achieved, the patient's sense of conviction is won, together with the therapeutic success that is dependent on it. [*BPP,* 39-40]

One further word is necessary, however, with respect to the therapeutic process. It is not enough to communicate to the patient an understanding of the aetiology and dynamics of his neurotic illness. Even when the communication is existential communication, another step is necessary, namely, the assimilation and inner appropriation of this knowledge. "The treatment," as Freud said elsewhere, "is made up of two parts, out of what the physician infers and tells the patient, and out of the patient's work of assimilation, or 'working through', what he hears" (*CP,* II, 286). This is a most essential aspect of the therapy. No therapy is complete unless this appropriation process has been thoroughly accomplished. "The first step in overcoming the resistance is made by the analyst's discovering the resistance, which is never recognized by the patient, and acquainting him with it" (*CP,* II, 375). But the second step is no less important.

One must allow the patient time to get to know this resistance of which he is ignorant, to 'work through' it, to overcome it, by continuing the work according to the analytic rule in defiance of it. Only when it has come to its height can one, with the patient's co-operation, discover the repressed instinctual trends which are feeding the resistance; and only by living them through in this way will the patient be convinced of their existence and their power.

> The physician has nothing more to do than to wait and let things take their course. [*CP*, II, 376]

Working through the resistances may indeed be a long and difficult process, but it is this process which effects the greatest change in the patient and insures lasting results.

In a sense there was no change whatever in the goal of therapy. Freud's aim, even from his very earliest efforts, was to recover the lost portion of the past which constitutes the self and from which the individual has become wholly alienated. It was always the intent of Freud's therapeutic methods to help the patient effect a "reconciliation with the repressed part of himself" (*CP*, II, 372). But the method of reaching that goal and Freud's understanding of what constitutes recollection were greatly modified. Recollection underwent a transmutation from a verbal recitation of the patient's personal history to an existential repetition of the dynamic meaning of that personal history. Even the "mood" of the therapeutic relationship changed greatly from that of the days of hypnotic suggestion, or even the days of free association. It seems apparent, then, that there took place in Freud's theory of therapy, even as I noted in his theories of neurosis and of the self, a marked trend from a fundamentally mechanistic viewpoint toward a more dynamic or dramatic one. Again it would seem that this represents a shift in Freud's fundamental orientation from naturalism toward historicism.

9. Interpolation: The Restoration of Selfhood

I turn now to the task of interpolating between Freud's and Kierkegaard's treatments of the therapeutic problem. While their analyses may appear to be widely disparate, the two men share a common concern. Each was preoccupied with the problem of the self and worked incessantly toward its resolution. To be sure, their language, methods, and tools were entirely different, but the consuming passion of each man, in his own way, was the restoration of selfhood.

For Kierkegaard there was only one problem: becoming a Christian. For him this was tantamount to becoming a self. The problem dominated virtually everything he wrote from the delightfully aesthetic *Either/Or* to the intensely religious *For Self-Examination. Philosophical Fragments* and its massive *Postscript,* perhaps the most influential of all his writings, were devoted exclusively to this problem (*PoV,* 10-43). With Kierkegaard this was no academic exercise; it was the distillate of his own life blood. His personal mode of existence was duplicated in his writings (*PoV,* 44-63). When he wrote *Fear and Trembling* in 1843, he was the "knight of infinite resignation," and he had become the "knight of faith" by the time he published *For Self-Examination* in 1851.

Similarly, the therapeutic problem dominated Freud's restless probing of the psychic depths of man—he was first and always a physician of the soul. It is a tribute to his infinite patience and disciplined compassion that he was able to disclose so much about the dynamics of the self and thereby to shed light upon the problems entailed in becoming a self. Kierkegaard's insights were almost exclusively autobiographical, and Freud's personal insights were supplemented by clinical experience. The data of each was existentially grounded.

The precipitate of Kierkegaard's spiritual odyssey was what he termed the "Christian therapeutic," while the result of Freud's endless hours of exploration within the depths of his patient's unconscious was the psychoanalytic method of therapy.

The Therapeutic Problem

Socrates, as Kierkegaard saw, is an appropriate starting point for understanding the problem of the self. Man's problem is that he does not know who he is. He cannot begin to become a self until he knows what it is that he is to become. So the problem is conceived to be fundamentally epistemological: How can one come to know the essence of his being? Socrates's resolution of this problem is his doctrine of recollection. He is convinced that man already possesses this knowledge; it is inherent in his being. The problem is that he has "forgotten" it. Consequently, the therapeutic task is to recall this forgotten truth, the essence or nature of man. Hence the therapeutic dictum: Know thyself. When, through recollection, one comes to know what he essentially is, the problem is in principle resolved. Ignorance is the cause of nonbeing, and knowing is tantamount to being.

Socrates's appraisal of the situation is all right so far as it goes, but it founders on the existential predicament of man. We are already in existence, and we must start existing our existence *without prior knowledge of the end.* We cannot suspend existence until we discover who we ought to be. If to make a beginning we must first know the end, we will never begin. This predicament, Kierkegaard observed, made an existentialist of Socrates, in spite of himself. He was forced to concede that *existence precedes essence.*

Freud begins where Socrates leaves off. Indeed, his thera-peutic method might well be construed as an existentialization of the Socratic doctrine of recollection. What Freud seeks to recollect, however, is not some "natural essence" of man but the "historical essence" of the individual. A man is his history, but ironically that history can become his prison. Freedom from this bondage to one's personal history is possible only when the individual has come to understand the dynamics of that history: the way in which the historical essence has come into being in the past and how it functions in the present. Therefore, Freud construes the Socratic dictum "Know thy-self" as an injunction to recollect one's personal history. Thus, where Socrates understood the therapeutic problem to be the recollection of a forgotten essence, Freud conceives it to be the recollection of a forgotten existence. This represents a marked advance beyond Socrates, but it stops short of its goal. Freud sees the existential problem which Socrates did not see, but his answer is not an existential answer.

It is precisely at this point that Kierkegaard goes beyond Freud. He seeks to give an existential answer to the existential problem, an answer treated under the rubric of repetition. Against Socrates, Kierkegaard would agree with Freud that the essence of man is an historical essence. But he would maintain that Freud's mode of recollection still functions on the ration-alistic level. Against Freud, as against Socrates, Kierkegaard insists that the problem is not essentially epistemological but existential. Knowledge, even of one's own historically acquired essence, if it remains extrinsic, does not restore the lost self-hood. Not only the content but the mode of knowing must be existential. What is required, Kierkegaard says, is not simply the recollection of one's history, but the repetition of that mode of being which is the creative source of that historical essence, namely historicity. The problem is seen to be not so much a matter of the recollection of a forgotten essence, how-ever historical, but a repetition of a lost existence. The thera-peutic problem, then, is how to bring about the repetition.

In summary: Socrates understands the problem to be the recollection of the eternal essence of man; Freud understands it to consist in the recollection of the historical essence of the individual; and Kierkegaard understands it to reside in the repetition of historicity.

The above characterization of Freud's understanding of the therapeutic problem is premature, however. Freud constantly revised his theory to accord with his empirical experience. He soon found that, while the historical essence of the individual is in principle accessible through the medium of memory, the task of recollecting this forgotten history is frustrated by a counterwill which blocks the recollection of painful memories. Freud encountered here the existential paradox which is far more pernicious than the epistemological paradox. The problem is not so much that the individual does not *know* the truth as that he *will* not know it. If knowledge of the historical essence is important, then willing to explore this history is crucial. It was this problem that Freud discovered and treated under the rubric of resistance. He learned that knowing does not always lead to doing. One may know the traumatic circumstances incident to the loss of selfhood and still remain in bondage to that history. Freud discovered that such knowledge was not therapeutic because it remained extrinsic to the self. What is required, he concluded, is an intrinsic appropriation of that knowledge. This constitutes a much more profound understanding of existential knowledge and represents a long step in the direction of Kierkegaard.

A concomitant of this shift in the locus of the therapeutic problem is a change in Freud's basic understanding of what constitutes existential truth. Beginning with what might be called an "objective" concept, he moves to a "subjective" conception of the truth of human existence. Again, this clearly seems to be a transition in the direction of Kierkegaard.

Kierkegaard gave classic expression to the existential understanding of truth in his formula "Truth is subjectivity." By this he meant that genuine human existence is radically subjective existence, that the authentic mode of man's existence is subjectivity. If the subjective mode of being is sacrificed, then man has lost his humanity. So fundamental is subjectivity that Kierkegaard is willing to relegate to a secondary importance the question of the "objective" truth. Another way of putting this is that truth is not an abstraction but a mode of being. This is the import of that often quoted assertion that "if only the mode of this relationship is in the truth, the individual is in the truth even if he should happen to be thus related to what is not true" (*CUP,* 178). By the same token, even if the individual is related to the truth, but that relationship remains an objective one, the individual is not in the truth. That is, the truth is not essentially related to his existence and therefore his existence is inauthentic. In short, the question of the how takes precedence over the question of the what; if *how* one is related to the truth is not valid, then *what* one is related to is immaterial.

As we have seen, Freud's early therapeutic work was premised on an objective conception of truth. His therapeutic efforts were bent upon disclosing the factual truth of the patient's life. To be sure, the truth for which he searched was historically acquired. I have termed it an "historical essence." But it was nonetheless objective. It could, with some justification, be construed as *Historie,* as opposed to *Geschichte*—an objective, external history as opposed to an internally appropriated meaning arising out of the historical event. Freud's concern was to help the patient arrive at an objective knowledge of this truth, to help him recover the forgotten facts of his personal history which have determined his present existence. If this could be accomplished, Freud was convinced the patient would be free. The emphasis here is evidently upon objectivity: an objective relation to an objective truth.

But, as we have also seen, Freud came to understand that this so-called objective truth is not always objective. The notable instance of this discovery occurred in the matter of infantile sexual experience. For a long time Freud premised his theory of neurosis upon the conviction that neurotic individuals have been subjected to some premature sexual experience, the reaction to which is determinative of the neurosis. His patients' dreams and recollections convinced him of this traumatic sexual aetiology. Therefore he made a considerable concession when he concluded that such "facts" are not objectively true, though they function as if they were. Thus, while this historical truth is not objective, it is nonetheless true. That is, it functions as the psychic truth of the patient's life. What is important, apparently, in regard to its truth, is the individual's relation to it—the relation makes it true for him. And this truth has to be taken as seriously as truth itself.

The complement of this discovery was the realization that objective knowledge of the truth is therapeutically useless. Freud began from the perspective that knowledge is tantamount to freedom, but he was forced to modify this notion. He found that one can impart to the patient the incontrovertible truth about the traumatic origin of his neurosis, but functionally this truth makes no difference. The patient continues to behave in his usual compulsive manner. Even when Freud modified his approach and supplanted information with interpretation, he was frustrated in his therapeutic aims. Apparently, even the most objective relationship to the historical truth of his being will not release the patient from his bondage to it, for this is not an objective-historical truth but a subjective-historical truth. It is not *Historie* but *Geschichte*.

The Therapeutic Method

This change in Freud's perspective had a profound effect upon his therapeutic method. When the problem was understood to be fundamentally organic in nature, various kinds of physical treatment were in order. When he came to appreciate the historical element in the neurosis, historical methods of treatment were required. But so long as Freud's naturalistic orientation limited his understanding of the historical to the objective-historical, his methods were confined to what Kierkegaard has called "direct communication"—the impartation of objective-historical information. As Freud came to appreciate the subjective dimension of the historical, however, new methods were demanded which could influence the subjective-historical situation of the patient.

Freud began his work as a neurologist, and his earliest therapeutic efforts followed the conventional neurological methods of the time. These were primarily physiological in character and included hot baths, massage, rest, and electrotherapy. But, as we have seen, Freud was not satisfied with the results of such methods. His study of the problem of neurosis soon led to a fundamental shift in his orientation—from a physiological to a psychological point of view. In effect his interest turned from neurology to psychology.

His new orientation was historical but deeply influenced by his naturalism. It was basically a naturalistic understanding of history. Freud called it a "traumatic" theory of neurosis. Here the emphasis was upon the objective event which was understood to be determinative of the illness. In keeping with the objective character of the causal event, Freud's therapeutic methods were objective. The goal of the therapy was to inform the patient about the precipitating event, and methods were developed appropriate to this goal. Hypnosis was employed to disclose the causal event and the physician's rapport with the patient was exploited to get him to accept the disclosure.

But with the gradual shift in Freud's orientation from the objective-historical to the subjective-historical came another change in method. We can observe the influence of this shift upon the therapeutic method in Freud's turning from hypnosis to free association. Hypnosis is basically an objective method of inquiry into the aetiology of the disease, while the free association method is a subjective approach. This shift is also apparent in the evolution of Freud's understanding of what the therapist contributes to the therapeutic process: from information to interpretation to participation in the transference neurosis. In the first stage, the therapist's relationship to the patient and the mode of communication are objective. In the therapy of interpretation the therapist is subjectively involved. He employs his powers of identification and empathy to comprehend the patient's secret and obtain his confirmation. In the transference method of therapy the physician permits himself to be drawn into the psychodrama of the neurotic's life in order to facilitate a subjective communication. Finally, we can recognize the influence of this shift in orientation upon the goals of therapy in the shift from recollection to repetition to "working through"—a shift which represents a successive existentialization of the doctrine of recollection. In the therapy of recollection the goal was to recall a forgotten event; in the therapy of "working through" the goal is to come to terms with the neurotic pattern of relationship and to incorporate the insight thus gained into the very fiber of one's existence.

Now while Kierkegaard never seriously entertained the option of an objective communication of information as a valid therapeutic method, his indirect method of communication does contain an element of objectivity. The "art," as he described it, "consists in reducing oneself, the communicator, to nobody, something purely objective" (*TiC,* 132). In practicing this art, Kierkegaard did not himself adopt a position but sought to reflect the position of the other, indeed, to accomplish a "double reflection" which neither condemned nor approved but forced the individual to decide for himself what judgment should be made of his own mode of being.

The parallel between Kierkegaard's method of indirect communication and Freud's method of free association is apparent from the following passages. First, Kierkegaard:

> As the psychological observer ought to be more agile than a tightrope dancer in order to be able to insinuate himself under the skin of other people and to imitate their attitudes, as his silence in confidential moments ought to be seductive and voluptuous in order that the hidden thing

may find pleasure in slipping out and chatting quietly with itself in this fictitious inattention and quiet, so he ought also to have a poetical primitiveness in his soul to be able to create at once the totality of the rule out of that which in the individual is always present. . . . The thing is to be quiet, silent, unobtrusive, so that one may lure the secret from him. Thereupon one practices what one has learned until one is able to deceive him. Thereupon one poetizes the passion and appears before him in passion's preternatural size. If this is done correctly, the individual will feel an indescribable relief and satisfaction, as does a demented man when one has found and poetically comprehended his fixed idea and then develops it further. [*CoD*, 49-50]

Freud's description of his method of free association reveals a strong similarity:

It was now a matter of regarding the material produced by the patient's associations as though it hinted at a hidden meaning and of discovering that meaning from it. Experience soon showed that the attitude which the analytical physician could most advantageously adopt was to surrender himself to his own unconscious mental activity, in a state of *easy and impartial attention,* to avoid so far as possible reflection and the construction of conscious expectations, not to try to fix anything that he heard particularly in his memory, and by these means to catch the drift of the patient's unconscious with his own unconscious. It was then found that, except under conditions that were too unfavorable, the patient's associations emerged like allusions, as it were, to one particular theme and that it was only necessary for the physician to go a step further in order to guess the material which was concealed from the patient himself and to be able to communicate it to him. [*CP*, V, 112]

The similarities are apparent, but perhaps it should be emphasized that both men employ an attitude of fictitious inattention or easy and impartial attention to disclose the hidden thing or hidden meaning of the person's life. Both then communicate what was hidden, or, as Kierkegaard would have it, poetize the passion in its preternatural size, so that the individual will recognize the fixed idea which dominates his life and find relief and satisfaction in this comprehension of himself.

But, while Kierkegaard favored this indirect method for the work of negation, he did not regard it as ultimately adequate to bring about the positive work of restoring selfhood. The indirect method may help the individual to be free from illusion, but it does nothing for establishing his relation to reality. For this aspect of the therapeutic task Kierkegaard insisted upon a radical subjectivity. The proclamation of the truth must be an existence-proclamation; it must be embodied in the one who seeks to communicate this truth. No stance of objectivity, no attitude of reflection will suffice—not even that of "double reflection." The communication of this truth can be accomplished only by "reduplication." The first movement of the spirit toward selfhood, resignation, may be brought about through the objective method; but the second movement, faith, can only be evoked in response to the subjective embodiment of truth in the therapist.

There is no doubt that Freud was moving in this direction in his ever evolving therapeutic practice. Certainly he traveled a long way from the direct communication of objective truth, which characterized his early therapeutic work, to the indirect communication of subjective truth which characterized his later approach. But, in spite of this significant shift in the direction of subjectivity, there remains a certain detachment or objectivity. To the end Freud was suspicious of "too much acting out" and of the countertransference which he felt could undermine therapeutic progress. If the therapist becomes too subjectively involved in the transference neurosis, he is unable to help the patient gain perspective and insight. Perhaps Freud was rightly cautious, at least insofar as the important work of negation is concerned, for there is always the danger that the therapist will be drawn into the sickness of the patient instead of drawing the patient out of his sickness into health.

Kierkegaard was also aware of the danger. He cautioned:

> [The witness] must, therefore, first get into touch with men. That is, he must begin with aesthetic achievement. This is earnest-money. The more brilliant the achievement, the better for him. Moreover he must be sure of himself, or (and this is the one and only security) he must relate himself to God in fear and trembling, lest the event most opposite to this intention should come to pass, and instead of setting the others in motion, the others acquire power over him, so that he ends by being bogged in the aesthetic. [*PoV*, 26]

Kierkegaard is saying here that, unless one's own selfhood is sustained by maintaining a relationship to the Power of selfhood, one is in danger of losing his self in the process of establishing communication with the aesthetic individual whom he seeks to help. But, while Kierkegaard is just as aware as Freud of the danger of losing one's own self in the subjective method of therapy, there is a decisive difference in their precautionary measures. Freud seeks to secure the identity of the therapist by retaining a measure of objectivity; Kierkegaard says that the one and only security is found in the relation of the self to God.

Thus it must be concluded that Sigmund Freud's great work is limited to the first and fundamental movement toward selfhood. Freud does not provide the final answer to the problem of the self since he only takes us up to the constructive task of selfhood. As Kierkegaard put it in the concluding lines of his study of dread, "So soon as psychology has finished with dread, it has nothing to do but to deliver it over to dogmatics"

(*CoD*, 145). It must be added, however, that this is no capitulation to objectivity. Kierkegaard's Christology remains radically subjective, as we shall see in the next section.

The Therapeutic Process

The preceding discussion of the therapeutic method could be characterized as an external view of the therapeutic process. Now an internal view, as it were, should be developed. What are the dynamics of the therapeutic process? What movements of the spirit, as Kierkegaard would put it, are required for the restoration of selfhood?

The problem, as Kierkegaard sees it, is that the individual is absolutely committed to relative ends and only relatively committed to the absolute end, i.e. selfhood. To translate this into the language of Freud, the ego is under the absolute domination of the superego and has thereby lost its executive function. The restoration to primacy of the absolute *telos,* selfhood, can only be accomplished by the prior resignation of the absolute relation to a relative *telos.* Again in Freudian language, the ego can only be restored to its executive function when its bondage to the superego has been broken. Kierkegaard and Freud are suggesting not the total renunciation of the relative norm but the recognition of its relativity in the establishment of a purely relative relationship to this norm.

Theologically, Kierkegaard would put it this way: the first movement toward the restoration of selfhood must be the renunciation of every relative *telos* which functions as a god. Psychologically, this is the renunciation of the domination of the self by the superego. That Freud understood the superego to function as a god is clearly indicated in his conviction that the god-concept is merely the projection of the father-image, i.e. the superego. So, for both Kierkegaard and Freud, the first step toward the restoration of selfhood is the renunciation of false gods or idols, or in Kierkegaard's words, resignation.

Neither Kierkegaard nor Freud is speaking about the renunciation of a rational ideal which operates only at the level of consciousness. Both are dealing with existentially operative motive forces. The *telos* of which Kierkegaard speaks is no less existentially ingrained than the neurotic patterns of behavior of which Freud speaks. So, when Kierkegaard refers to the resignation of relative *teloi* for the sake of an absolute *telos*, he does not mean a rational, deliberate changing of the mind with respect to just which ideal among many is the summum bonum. He refers to a radical change in the motivational core of one's being. This change is not easily accomplished, for to renounce one's god is to relinquish the very core of one's being. Even if this god is his demon, the individual clings to it with the desperation born of dread. It determines his destiny; it is his fate, his self. Hence resignation cannot be accomplished without deep psychic suffering, the suffering of a self which is required to give up its self in order to find its self.

Just how much suffering Freud well knew. In some respects Freud's exploration of what Kierkegaard calls "resignation" is much more exhaustive and definitive than Kierkegaard's, not in principle but in its detail and specificity. Perhaps no one has expressed so well and so profoundly as Kierkegaard what is required of the self if it is to become a self. But similarly no one has documented that journey through dread so well and so exhaustively as Freud. What Kierkegaard lacks in clinical breadth Freud supplies; and what Freud lacks in theological depth Kierkegaard supplies.

Freud's therapeutic work is a clinical documentation of the way of resignation, the painful process of liberating the self from its bondage to the past. It is not so much the events of the past with which one has to come to terms but the existential meaning of the events, the shaping of the very character structure of the self which took place in these events. To face up to the anxiety-producing circumstances which brought about the neurotic character structure is a painful experience since this recollection evokes again the dread which precipitated the original response. Furthermore, Freud came to see that to rectify this neurotic response not just recollection but existential recollection or repetition is required. And this entails no small amount of suffering.

The ultimate suffering, however, is what Kierkegaard calls *Anfechtung*. This is the suffering of the limit situation. The closer one comes to authentic selfhood, subjectivity, the more intense becomes the dread. There is a limit to man's capacity for dread. *Anfechtung* represents the expression of that limit. Freud also recognizes this phenomenon. He treats it under the category of resistance. The closer one comes to the core of the problem, the greater becomes the resistance. The resistance to cure stems from the same source as the original repression, namely, anxiety or dread. Just as the dread arising from an existential situation brought about the flight from selfhood, so the dread which increases with the approximation of the same situation sustains the repression through resistance to therapy.

Kierkegaard's resolution of the problem is dialectical; Freud's is dualistic. For Kierkegaard, man lives out his existence in the creative tension between Spirit and dread, between the desire for selfhood and the dread of selfhood. For Freud, life is a continual conflict between Eros and Thanatos. Caught in his ontological dualism, the best Freud could offer was a compromise between Eros and Thanatos brought about through sublimation.

But, as Kierkegaard points out, while accepting the limit situation is the only possible human response, it is still existence in guilt. The relationship to the ultimate *telos* of one's existence will always be a disrelationship, and this disrelationship is guilt. In this situation, the most authentic attitude would therefore be guilt-consciousness, the consciousness that one is himself responsible for the disrelationship. To accept this guilt, this basic responsibility for one's being, is the kind of fundamental choice which makes possible guilt and innocence with respect to all relative matters. This guilt is much more fundamental than the external guilt of civil law or even the internal guilt of conscience. It is precisely that level of guilt which makes possible these other levels of guilt. And, conversely, it is the kind of guilt the acceptance of which makes innocence possible on the other levels.

Freud is pointing to this guilt when he seeks to free men from the guilt of the superego type. He is seeking not to abrogate responsibility but to restore responsibility at the fundamental level of selfhood. Rather than condoning the capitulation of moral freedom to a culturally relative *telos,* Freud is seeking to restore to man that freedom which is the real root of guilt and innocence. If the individual can be brought to accept responsibility for his existence—to be essentially guilty as Kierkegaard put it—innocence and guilt become meaningful categories, and forgiveness becomes an existential possibility.

Thus the first movement in the restoration of selfhood is resignation, which involves deep psychic suffering and ultimately guilt. This is the work of negation, the task of extricating the self from its bondage to false gods. But the work of negation does not complete the restoration of the self. Freedom is a neutral mode of being. To be sure, it is fundamental. Without it there can be no genuine selfhood. But when freedom is secured the individual must *in freedom* choose what self he will become. He must choose the *telos* of his life.

This is the positive work of therapy. The self must posit itself with respect to that *telos* which it now chooses to be ultimate. About this Freud has nothing to say. His therapeutic work can free the self from its bondage to the superego, but it cannot specify to what end the self is free. In short, psychoanalysis is theologically neutral. Indeed, within the limits of a naturalistic perspective this is all it can legitimately contribute. Nature cannot designate man's god, for man is an historic creature and his god is an historic reality. Only history can reveal to man his god.

After the work of negation is completed, the work of position remains. This is the area where Kierkegaard makes his most significant contribution to our understanding of the therapeutic process. He insists that the God who transcends the culturally relative god of the superego is the God who revealed himself in Christ. He is the God who is wholly other than every finite god, and who remains wholly other even in his revelation in the Christ event. What is revealed in Christ is the God-Man relationship, a mode of being in which the ultimate relationship which constitutes true selfhood is sustained. In Christ is revealed the God-Man relationship—the relationship of a self which is absolutely related to the God who is wholly other than every concrete image of him. In the subjective relationship of faith, the God who is wholly other is profoundly present without being reduced to an objective and hence relative god.

To be sure, man's historic relationship to such a God has left a cultural precipitate which functions as our god. And Freud has elucidated the psychodynamics of the relationship of man to such a god. But every such god is a relative god. The God revealed in the God-Man relationship of the Christ, however, is the God who absolutely transcends the culturally acquired image of himself. He is that Reality who continually calls us to transcend ourselves, who calls us out of our bondage to the past and its precipitate gods to exist in freedom. When the work of negation is accomplished we must not simply substitute one finite god for another. We must not adopt some new ideology to supplant the father-image god with which we have become disillusioned. We must, in faith, relate ourselves to the God who absolutely transcends the cultural precipitate of his historical encounter with men.

The paradigm of such a way of being is Jesus Christ. Through our faith response he becomes the ideal image of selfhood, the absolute *telos,* the end of our existence. Confronted with such a being our nonbeing is clearly exposed. But now it is no longer a general nonbeing but a specific nonbeing; and guilt-consciousness, a moral category, is transformed to sin-consciousness, an ontological category.

And how is sin-consciousness overcome? Only by the faith response. When one responds in faith to the God revealed in the Christ event, he is freed from sin through that response. Since sin is unfaith, then the concomitant of faith is the forgiveness of sin. Sin is a disrelationship in the relation of the self to the Power which posits selfhood. The faith response is the confession of that disrelationship. But in the confession the relationship is established, and the establishment of the relationship is tantamount to forgiveness. Faith is a paradoxical mode of being. By faith one is continually made conscious of his bondage and simultaneously made free. Existence in faith is the paradoxical existence of the forgiven sinner.

Selfhood is therefore that mode of being which sustains a relative relation to the relative *teloi* and an absolute relation to the absolute *telos*. This requires the continual double movement of the Spirit: resignation and faith. It requires the continual renunciation of the idols of the mind, which constitute a bondage to an ideology, together with the continual reaffirmation of the relationship to that Power within us which transcends all such idols and is therefore the Power which imparts freedom to the Spirit in spite of dread.

10. Conclusion: Implications for Psychotherapy and Theology

The projected study is now complete, and it has produced some surprising results. It is clear that, in spite of the radically disparate perspectives from which Kierkegaard and Freud view the phenomena of selfhood, their insights are strikingly similar. Where they differ they seem to supplement rather than contradict one another. Since the interpolations at the end of each section have sought to correlate these insights, no further comment is necessary to show the relationship of the two interpretations of the self. But perhaps it would be helpful, by way of conclusion, to point up the significance of this study for both psychotherapy and theology.

Implications for Psychotherapy

Freud's psychoanalytical theories have been under attack from their inception. But current criticism cannot be dismissed as lightly as Freud dismissed the criticism of his own day, much of which stemmed from ignorance, prejudice, and Victorian prudery. Contemporary criticism arises in a post-Freudian culture and often comes from therapists who have received extensive training in the psychoanalytic method. The criticisms basically cluster around the three concepts which form the structure of this study: the concept of the self, the concept of neurosis, and the concept of therapy.

Many critics maintain that Freud's concept of the self really eliminates the self. His great emphasis upon the unconscious tends to obscure the importance of the conscious aspect of the self. The ego becomes, at best, a broker between the irrational drives which emerge from the id and the prohibitions of the superego, both of which function largely at the unconscious level. The ego is lived by the id more than vice versa. Consequently, the conscious, rational, deliberative functions which are ordinarily considered to be the essence of selfhood are replaced by what is basically a deterministic interpretation.

Freud is also frequently criticized for his reductionistic pansexualism. In place of the sex drive critics have posited a general life urge (Jung), a drive for power (Adler), a quest for meaning (Frankl), a need for security (Horney, Sullivan), or a power to be (Binswanger). Each in his own way rejects as too simplistic the reduction of the diverse phenomena of selfhood to libidinal manifestations.

A corollary of this rejection of Freud's Libido theory is the rejection of the theory of neurosis based upon it. Clara Thompson has noted that Freud construes as constitutional much that is simply cultural in origin. The neuroses arising from the Oedipal conflict and the repression of Libido are a case in point. As many psychoanalysts have noted, the passing of Victorian culture has reduced the incidence of classical Freudian neuroses. Frankl particularly insists that he rarely encounters the libidinal neurosis which so dominated Freud's research. The predominant neuroses now are what he terms *noögenic neuroses,* i.e. neuroses arising from a crisis of meaninglessness (not from a libidinal crisis). The experiences of other therapists are similar, though some would characterize contemporary neuroses more in terms of a breakdown in interpersonal relations (Horney, Sullivan), or a flight from freedom (Fromm).

Finally, criticism focuses upon Freud's therapeutic methods. The failure of classical psychoanalytic methods to bring about a high incidence of cures and the extensive investment of time involved in the therapeutic process, were the factors which, more than any others, forced therapists who were trained in

Freud's methods to reconsider his presuppositions. The emphasis in analysis has shifted from the extensive recapitulation of the patient's personal history to the present or even the future. And greater emphasis has been put on the interpersonal relationship between therapist and patient.

Freud was aware of the limitations of his theory and he attempted to correct them. We have seen this in the movement of his theory from the somatic to the psychological to the metapsychological and in the transmutation of Libido into Eros. It is apparent in his shift of interest from id to ego psychology and, in the aetiology of neurosis, from constitutional to cultural factors. It is also evident in the evolution of his understanding of the role of the therapist from informant to interpreter to participant in the transference neurosis of the patient. And finally it is implicit in the shift in his understanding of truth from objectivity to subjectivity. But Freud's fundamental naturalism proved to be an inadequate framework for these insights.

I would maintain that Freud's limitations arose from an inadequate ontological foundation. His whole approach to the problem of the self is grounded in a naturalistic ontology, whereas the phenomena of selfhood are essentially historical. To be sure, his naturalism is vitalistic; it is not the rationalistic naturalism of most nineteenth-century psychology. Freud sought to interpret the phenomena of selfhood in terms of the dynamics of Libido, the vital power or essence of the self, instead of in terms of rational essences. But the essentially naturalistic model which emerged was inadequate to the historical reality it sought to comprehend.

It is my contention that an historical ontology would provide a more adequate basis for psychoanalysis.[1] An historical ontology assumes that the fundamental category is *becoming* rather than *being,* history instead of nature, existence not essence. The nature of man is to create his own nature. A man

1. Brown, *Life Against Death,* especially chap. 7.

is his history. Most existential psychoanalysis is grounded on this concept, and the change in ontological commitment has required a change in theory and in therapeutic methods. The revision of psychoanalysis by the existentialists has, however, been accomplished only at the sacrifice of some of Freud's most perceptive insights. Most have rejected the Libido theory entirely, along with the concept of the unconscious, and the theory that the patient's past experiences have a determinative effect. This is too great a price to pay. It discards the hard-won gains of classical psychoanalysis with its insights into the depth dimension of the self, to return to the relatively shallow, rationalistic and voluntarist understanding of the nineteenth-century.

Some, it is true, strive to be eclectic, applying Freudian psychoanalysis to certain kinds of neuroses, and existential psychoanalysis to others. But this is premature. It is eclectic without truly integrating the id psychology with the ego psychology. It fails to resolve the fundamental ontological question. While there is a certain pragmatic utility to this approach, theoretically it is unacceptable. There must yet be found a unifying theory of the self which brings about a genuine synthesis of psychoanalysis and existential analysis.

Kierkegaard's historical ontology provides the basis for just such a synthesis. The essence of being is becoming and history is the fundamental ontological category. The essential meaning of things lies not in the past but in the future. But, against those who have sought to apply this insight to psychoanalysis, we must note that Kierkegaard's historical ontology does not abrogate nature; it historicizes it. Nature is a "first becoming" which provides the framework for the "second becoming" we call history. In actuality, even the first becoming is historical. It is simply that history which has already transpired; it is that becoming which has already come into being. What we call "nature" was once itself historical; it is the present stage of the historical process called evolution. What we call "human nature" is simply the precipitate of human history. It possesses the stability of the past which has already become, and can therefore, with some justification, be comprehended in naturalistic categories. But it also participates in a history which has not yet transpired, and to this extent it transcends the naturalistic categories. Freud's vitalistic naturalism seeks to take into account the historical dimension of human existence, but it does so with only limited success. Current existential psychoanalysis, on the other hand, errs in ignoring the dialectical character of history. History is always a dialectical relationship between being and becoming; between the past and the future; or, put in Kierkegaard's terms, between necessity and possibility. Freudian psychoanalysis ignores possibility, while existential psychoanalysis ignores necessity. A synthesis is possible only on the basis of a genuine dialectical ontology. This Kierkegaard supplies. On the basis of such an ontology the processes which Freud interpreted naturalistically can be reconstructed.

From this study of Kierkegaard and Freud the outline of a genuinely existential psychoanalysis has emerged. In the doctrine of Spirit as the power of being, the charge of pansexualism is avoided without sacrificing Freud's insight into the centrality of the Libido in the phenomena of selfhood. In Kierkegaard's concept of the self, an ego psychology is posited which does not abrogate the depth dimension out of concern for the sublime, but which is dialectically related to the id psychology of Freud. On the basis of Kierkegaard's historical ontology a genuine freedom is accorded the self, without ignoring the determinism of historical choice. Noögenic neuroses are comprehended within the same theoretical framework as the transference neuroses. And the relationship between classical psychoanalytic and existential methods of therapy is clarified.

With respect to the power of selfhood, we have seen how Kierkegaard's doctrine of Spirit subsumes Freud's doctrine of the Libido. Spirit is the inherent drive toward selfhood or self-determination. But this is not to deny the significance of the sexual. Indeed, perhaps the earliest manifestation of Spirit is to be found in the emergence of the sex drive. Far from rejecting Libido, then, such an existential psychoanalysis would acknowledge it as a primitive expression of Spirit, which undergoes successive historicization or sublimation—first as Eros, then as Philia, and finally as Agape, its most sublime manifestation.

The existentialization of the theory of the ego is commensurate with the above. The ego is the historical product of Spirit. The mode of selfhood manifested is a function of the way in which the self relates itself to Spirit, the power of its being. Insofar as the self assumes an immediate relation to Spirit in its primitive libidinal manifestation and is lived by the libidinal drives instead of assuming responsibility for them, the self is a pleasure-ego or id. But, when the self assumes responsibility for the libidinal drive and relates it to reality, a new mode of selfhood emerges coincident with the manifestation of a more sublime form of Spirit. Here the reality-ego or simply the ego emerges, and Spirit manifests itself as Philia. Ultimately Spirit emerges in its most sublime form, Agape, and the structure in which the self seeks to incorporate the ideal is the ideal-ego or superego.

The theory of neurosis has also undergone an existentialization. Loss of selfhood is not confined to that form which is due to the repression of the Libido, though this does indeed account for the transference neuroses. Selfhood can also be lost through rejecting reality. This is the phenomenon of psychosis. And selfhood can be lost through the denial of ideality. This is the locus of the noögenic neuroses.

Finally, there is the existentialization of the therapeutic theory. While it is true that genuine selfhood consists in its historicity, it is also true that the history it creates can become its prison. Consequently, therapy is not simply the task of liberating the self from its bondage to history; it is also the task of restoring to the self is essential historicity. Therapy requires not just the negative work of resignation, the coming to terms with guilt occasioned at the level of finite meanings. It also requires the positive work of faith, the coming to terms with sin occasioned at the level of ultimate meaning. Thus, the necessary correlate of psychoanalysis is existential analysis, or what is called "existential psychoanalysis."

To be sure, this is merely suggestive of what would constitute a genuine existentialization of psychoanalysis, but it does provide an agenda for the task.

Implications for Theology

The history of Christian thought is a history of the conflict between reason and revelation, a conflict as old as the encounter between Athens and Jerusalem. When Christianity penetrated the Greek culture, it attempted to communicate its insights in the naturalistic categories of Greek thought. But whether its attempts took Platonic or Aristotelian form there was always vigorous protest from those who insisted the Christian perspective is not amenable to a naturalistic interpretation. Sometimes the protest took the form of mysticism, sometimes pietism. But it always took the form of supernaturalism whose epistemology was based on revelation, not reason.

To be sure, the "medieval synthesis" accorded a place to each, but it was never really a synthesis. It was an ad hoc solution in which revelation was added to reason although there is no essential relationship between the two. The breakdown of the medieval synthesis polarized the debate once again: first in terms of Catholic scholasticism versus Protestant fideism; and then in terms of Protestant scholasticism versus sectarian pietism. In the first part of this century the debate was manifested in the conflict between liberalism and orthodoxy. Liberalism's attempt to ground theology in rationalistic idealism has been termed a "splendid failure," but fundamentalism's defense of orthodoxy was no more successful. So it was with great expectations that the theological world saw the issue joined by Tillich and Barth on somewhat more satisfactory grounds. Tillich's thought is the epitome of naturalistic theology, while Barth's monumental work presents supernaturalism at its finest. At the height of the debate, however, there has emerged a movement which says, in effect, a plague on both your houses! The God hypothesis is no longer tenable whether in its rationalistic or its fideistic form. God is dead, and we must live in the painful awareness of his absence.

But the supernaturalistic response to naturalistic theology creates a false dichotomy. The alternative to naturalism is not supernaturalism but historicism. The problem with naturalistic theology is not its dependence upon reason but its use of the wrong kind of reason. Theology's logic is historical reason, not natural reason. And this error will not be corrected by an appeal to the irrational. The death of God theology simply begs the question. In both Altizer's and Hamilton's versions, it is simply a secular form of fideism. It takes either the form of mysticism (Altizer), or the form of pietism (Hamilton), if indeed it does not take the form of ordinary atheism. What is needed is a theology which avoids the error of naturalistic theology without resorting to fideism in either its supernaturalistic or its positivistic form. Kierkegaard provides the basis for just such a theology. On the basis of his historical ontology there can be constructed a theology which fully explicates the existential reality of the Christian faith. Of course, both Barth and Tillich attempted to do just that, though in radically different ways. Each is, in a sense, a Kierkegaardian; but each has failed to sustain the dialectic which Kierkegaard perceived.

Barth's failure stems from a one-sided response to the challenge of Kierkegaard. Barth picked up the transcendental end of the Kierkegaardian dialectic but ignored the immanental. He emphasized the wholly otherness of God at the expense of his presence. He rejected as idolatrous every attempt of reason to comprehend the nature of God and hence was driven to a supernaturalistic epistemology. To be sure, Barth preserved one "point of contact" between God and man, for without

such there could be no knowledge of God at all. But he es-
chewed any attempt to justify his Christological epistemology
save one, the leap of faith. Unfortunately, Kierkegaardian
theology has come to be identified with this Barthian muta-
tion, but to do so is to ignore the full dialectic of the infinite
and the finite.

Tillich has erred in the opposite direction. He has, perhaps,
come nearer to preserving Kierkegaard's dialectical method,
but his theology eliminates the historical dimension. His is a
dialectic of tension, not a developmental dialectic. It is static
rather than dynamic. This is because the primary category of
his ontology is being, not becoming. Being itself is comprised
of polar elements in dialectical tension, but there is no pro-
cess-character to the dialectic. Being itself does not change,
and, since for Tillich God is being itself, God is not himself
historical. He is not in any literal sense a "living" God.[2] In the
end Tillich capitulates to essentialism, as he himself admits.[3]

The question might well be raised whether Tillich's or, for
that matter, anyone's attempt to develop systematic theology
on an existential base is not bound to fail. After all it was
Kierkegaard himself who said that "an existential system is
impossible" (*CUP*, 107ff). But the point of Kierkegaard's assertion is not the irrationality of existence, but the error in
assuming that existence can be comprehended by the categories of essentialistic reason. There is in Kierkegaard an implicit ontology, but it is historical not naturalistic. It is an
ontology which focuses on becoming, not being, an ontology
which seeks to articulate the rationale of existence in which
genuine creation is possible, an ontology which gives significance to that which history creates. Just as Kierkegaard never
developed this ontology, he never developed a theology. Either
task would have been foreign to his concern. But the out-

2. Paul Tillich, *Systematic Theology* (Chicago: University of Chicago
Press, 1951), 1: 242.
3. Paul Tillich, "On the Boundary Line," *Christian Century* (Decem-
ber 7, 1960): 1437.

lines of a theology grounded in an historical ontology are discernible.

Such a theology has its origin in anthropology, for human existence is intrinsically historical. The self is not an eternal essence which develops with natural necessity. Rather, the self emerges in an explicitly historical manner. It comes into being as a free response to the possibilities present in its given situation, and it continues to become only insofar as it sustains this dialectical relationship with possibility. But the moment in which that choice is made is itself the product of prior historical decisions. Hence, the range of possibilities present in any given moment are never infinite and the freedom is never absolute. However, since the moving moment which is the present continually discloses new aspects of a seemingly inexhaustible possibility, the dialectic of selfhood is a dialectic between the finite, temporal necessity of the past and the infinite, eternal possibility which is the future.

Infinite, eternal possibility is what Kierkegaard means by Spirit. Hence, Spirit is the fundamental category in an historical theology. Spirit is the power of human being, because without it the dialectic of selfhood would collapse. It exercises a god-function in the dialectic of the self; it is the absolute *telos* of human existence—the always transcendent, utterly inexhaustible horizon of the self. It is the creative source of human being, the Godhead.

This is what it means to speak of God as "creator." God, or Spirit, projects its own reality—infinite, eternal possibility—before the individual, thereby calling the self into existence. But this creation is historical. It transpires in freedom and only by virtue of the response of the individual. It is true that without the presence of Spirit selfhood would be impossible, but the free response of the individual is equally essential. The self is not an object, objectively produced, but a subject, subjectively created. The process whereby it comes into being is commensurate with the end. The subject can only become a subject, subjectively.

Therefore, the creative work of the Holy Spirit is both a call and a response.

By virtue of the freedom which is present in the creative process of the Spirit, the self may fail to become a self. And, by virtue of the necessities of its historical situation and the overwhelming terror of absolute possibility, the self will not become a self. There is a flight from freedom, a denial of Spirit, with a consequent loss of selfhood. This is the existential rationale of the doctrine of the Fall.

But, even in the fallen state, the power of selfhood functions to restore to the self its selfhood. Even in the self's greatest extremity, Spirit manifests itself as the possibility which appears when every possibility has been swallowed up in necessity. Thus, Spirit not only creates the self but continually recreates it. Spirit continually provides a new occasion for selfhood, even when the self has lost its selfhood. This is the existential significance of the doctrine of redemption.

As one would expect, historical theology is also more effective than naturalistic theology in elucidating the Judeo-Christian perception of God as the God of history, indeed as one who acts in history. Under the categories of a naturalistic theology this perception was construed after the model of a divine puppeteer. "God acts in history" was construed to mean that a supernatural being controlled the historical process. The "hard form" of this doctrine understood every event to be the will of God; the "soft form" preferred to speak only of certain special acts of divine intervention into an otherwise free historical process. The former required continual qualification of the will of God until rationality vanished in inscrutability. The latter qualified the power of God until omnipotence disappeared in caprice. Both constitute the "death by a thousand qualifications" to which Anthony Flew refers.[4] What had died, of course, is not God but a specific model

4. A. Flew and A. MacIntyre, *New Essays in Philosophical Theology* (New York: Macmillan Company, 1955), p. 107.

which has proven to be inadequate to the historical reality it sought to explicate.

Historical theology encounters no such difficulty. God acts in history as the absolute *telos*, Spirit. He creates history through man's response to the reality of Spirit. But there is no necessity for this response to be a faithful response. When it is, it is what biblical scholars call *Heilsgeschichte* and what the prophets referred to as the "mighty acts of God." When the response is unfaithful to the Holy Spirit, the result is said to be "demonic." But even in the darkest hours of history, Spirit is present as possibility, which can redeem the time—but only *historically*, that is, through the free response of men.

The above constitutes the rough outlines of a doctrine of the Holy Spirit which is grounded in an historical ontology. Spirit is the power of human being, the creative source of selfhood, and the *telos* of history. Thus far, however, we have considered the concept of Spirit only with regard to the phenomena of the self. Nothing has been said of the relation of Spirit to the so-called natural phenomena. Kierkegaard himself provides the basis for an extrapolation from the concept of Spirit as the power of human being to the more comprehensive notion of Spirit as the power of being itself, from anthropology to cosmology. The basis for this extension of existential thought is found in Kierkegaard's notion of the two becomings. The preceding discussion has concerned itself with the second becoming, the explicitly historical becoming which transpires in freedom. That is, the historical processes take place as the free response of individuals to the range of possibilities available in a given historically determined situation.

The natural processes are usually thought to transpire with necessity. But, for Kierkegaard, the first becoming or natural becoming is also historical in character. It lends itself to the naturalistic interpretation, because it represents a becoming which has already become. What we call "nature" is the product of historical processes which have reached a relatively stable stage of development. Nevertheless, the process by means of which the present mode of being has evolved is itself historical. Under the given historical conditions, the evolutionary species was presented with infinite, eternal possibilities. No eternal essence or nature determined which of the possibilities would be actualized. In the process of what is called "natural" selection, many of the possibilities were actualized as mutations, but the context of coincident historical processes which made up its environment determined which of the possibilities thus actualized would endure.

Thus, on the level of nàture, the same dialectic of Spirit is present—the dialectic of infinite, eternal possibility with finite, temporal necessity. And, within the relatively stable structures which have emerged from this process, that dialectic continues. Here historicity is manifest more as a repetition of a satisfactory mode of being than as the innovation of new modes of being. But even within this attenuated historicity freedom and possibility are present, and necessity is not absolute. Thus, Spirit is present as the power of being itself, and the historical doctrine of creation is extended to nature as well as to man.

We must now move from the concept of the Holy Spirit to the notion of God the Father. This is a movement from the abstract to the concrete, from the absolute to the relative, from the transcendent to the immanent. Spirit, as the absolute *telos* of man, gives little specific guidance to the individual in his quest for selfhood. It may call the individual into selfhood, but it does not inform the self with specific content or values. To be relevant, the Absolute must take on specificity. This it does through the historical process itself.

Spirit projects its own reality, which is infinite, eternal possibility. This is an overwhelming *telos;* it staggers the imagination. But it lacks specificity. The self cannot begin to become a self without some concrete image of the self it is to be. This imagination supplies. By means of the imagination the abstract becomes concrete, the absolute becomes relative, God is imaged. The Godhead becomes a god through the instrumentality of the religious imagination, and the *telos* of the self becomes specific in an ideal image of the self. The coincidence of the problem of God and the problem of the self is grounded in this fact: the identity of the self is dependent upon the identity of its God.

Freud has clarified the process whereby the father-image of God is acquired. He has shown that the concept of God as Father arises from the process of identification. Through the identification of the child with his father he receives an ideal image of the self. This ideal self or superego is an idealized version of his earthly father, and it functions as his God. The voice of conscience is experienced as the voice of God. Its dictates carry the weight of a divine imperative, for they are inherent in the very structure of the self.

It goes without saying that this God is not identical with Absolute Spirit. Derived from culture and historically relative, this God is at best an approximation of Spirit. Its imperative is only relatively valid. It is the historical precipitate of the dialectic of Spirit, and hence possesses a certain validity. But it also embodies the finite, the temporal, and the necessary, and so is only relatively valid.

There is no necessity for the patriarchal character of the image of God. In a matriarchal society the image may well be that of a Mother-God. Indeed, a strong tendency in this direction is manifested in some cultures in the popularity of the worship of Mary as the Mother of God. It is entirely conceivable that the image of God could be manifested in a form which is neither patriarchal nor matriarchal, as indeed is the case in the "atman" concept of the Hindu religion.

We should also note that such an understanding of the historical process whereby the Absolute Spirit becomes a relative god, is the basis of the notion of a living God. While the Holy Spirit is absolute—i.e. infinite, eternal possibility—God the Father is relative. He is subject to the relativities of history and the culture it produces. The God-concept, then, is itself historical. It is itself subject to the dialectic of Spirit and to the corrective of history.

The concept of revelation is also grounded in this understanding of the historicity of the God-concept. Revelation is the dialectic of imagination. The Holy Spirit continually discloses itself through the historical evolution of its image. Through the religious imagination new insight into the implications of Spirit for selfhood is preserved in the evolving image of God. Thus, the knowledge of God is the subjective knowledge of conscience. It is a "knowing-with" which is prior to the subject-object dichotomy of objective knowledge. It is a knowledge in which the object is also subject, for the knowledge of God is the knowledge of self in the coincidence of self and God.

Finally, let us turn to the third person of the Trinity, to which we are driven by the relativity of the second. The religion of the Father is ultimately an adolescent religion. In the dialectic of selfhood the self finds its identity through a relationship with its ideal-ego or its God. But the self for whom this relative image of the Spirit, the Godhead, is absolute, is a self which has lost its selfhood. It is in bondage to a culturally relative God; it is in bondage to its superego. This image of God is not God but an idol, as the Hebrew religious insight perceived. The Godhead cannot be imaged; hence the prohibition against graven images. Nor can it be conceptualized; hence the name which is given Moses—"I will become who I will become." The religion of the Father is a religion of guilt. It is the religion of Law, a superego religion.

The religion of the Son emancipates the self from the religion of the Father; it frees the self from the Law to live according to the Spirit. In the religion of the Son, Christ is not a new image of God but an image of the Self. Christ is the paradigm of selfhood, the dialectical incarnation of God. In him is fully manifest the dialectic of the finite and the infinite, the temporal and the eternal, necessity and possibility. In short, he is the paradigm of the relationship between man and God. As such, Kierkegaard calls him the God-Man.

He is the Way, the Truth, and the Life. He is the Way to

selfhood, for he exemplifies the double movement of the Spirit; the way of resignation and faith; the way of renouncing the tyranny of the relative for the emancipation of the absolute Spirit. He is the Truth, in Kierkegaard's sense of the word, for his relationship to the Spirit is one of passionate subjectivity. And he is the Life, for he is the existential embodiment of Spirit. In him the dialectic of the Spirit has found its most sublime manifestation, Agape, beyond Eros and Philia. As such he has the capacity to inspire (en-spirit) the self to become a self, to engage in the dialectic of the Spirit which is selfhood.

Index